THE LAND WITHOUT A BANKING LAW

THE LAND WITHOUT A BANKING LAW

How to Start a Bank with a Thousand Dollars

MICHAEL MAGNUSSON

Published By:
OPUS OPERIS LLP
Regency House—Westminster Place
York—YO26 6RW—United Kingdom

Registered in the United Kingdom with Company Number OC381062

OPUS
OPERIS

We plant a new tree for every printed book we sell.
See www.opusoperis.co.uk for further details.

ISBN: 978-0-9575438-1-2

*"If it would not look too much like showing off,
I would tell the reader where New Zealand is."*

From "Following the Equator" by Mark Twain

CONTENTS

LEGAL NOTICE

"The first European to find it was a Dutch sea-captain who was looking for something else, and who thought it a part of South America, from which it is sundered by five thousand miles of ocean. It takes its name from a province of Holland to which it does not bear the remotest likeness, and is usually regarded as the antipodes of England, but is not. Taken possession of by an English navigator, whose action, at first adopted, was afterwards reversed by his country's rulers, it was only annexed at length by the English Government which did not want it, to keep it from the French who did. The Dominion's capital bears the name of a famous British commander, whose sole connection with the country was a flat refusal to aid in adding it to the Empire."

From "Long White Cloud" by William Pember Reeves

INTRODUCTION

New Zealand Offshore Finance Companies are Banks, both in a legal and practical sense, but not Registered Banks under the supervision of the Reserve Bank of New Zealand. These entities have become a controversial subject during the past few years. They have also been a target for anti-offshore bloggers and would-be journalists. If one were to believe certain bloggers, the only reason one could possibly have to establish an international banking business in New Zealand would be to commit fraud or to launder funds from criminal activities. It is quite remarkable how gossip and speculation on the Internet can spin totally out of control and how audacious bloggers never hesitate to attack entire business sectors, companies and individuals without possessing the slightest knowledge of the subject at hand. Conspicuously, certain bloggers are often found to accuse pretty much anyone who does business offshore of hiding behind intricate corporate structures and nominee directors, while they themselves hide behind aliases and pseudonyms when making their unlearned and unfounded accusations.

Despite some widespread beliefs, the offshore sector is not in decline, quite to the contrary. In a global economy where borders are becoming increasingly invisible, businesses small and large, and especially those doing business on the Internet, sooner or later get faced with decisions involving jurisdictional selection.

Offshore simply means outside the country of residence. So when the US Company Dell set up a call center in Panama this is considered an offshore operation. Likewise when PepsiCo set up their holding company in Denmark to enjoy tax-free dividends or when Apple use reseller agreements with their own low tax Irish offshore company to limit taxable profits in other European markets. There is nothing unusual or suspicious about this. Taxation is a cost of doing business like any other for a corporation, and so is regulatory compliance. Corporations make money (their primary purpose) by generating revenues and controlling costs and they do this by choosing the most suitable jurisdiction for each aspect of their operation. Some may find it suspicious that more than 50% of all publicly traded corporations in the United States and more than 60% of the Forbes 500 Companies happen to be incorporated in the tiny US state of Delaware. Clearly there are legitimate strategic reasons for this just as there are for Apple to manufacture iPads and iPhones in China rather than in California.

Cross border corporate structuring is a booming business. I think it will always remain so too, unless of course we one day end up with a single nation planet with one single tax rate and a single set of laws and regulations. Images of a world where we all walk around in identical uniforms and address each other by global identity number rather than by name come to mind. Until then, corporations and international entrepreneurs will reap the benefits that each country has when selecting where to structure legal entities, just as they consider labor costs when choosing the location for a new factory.

When PayPal decided to structure their Company serving non-US and non-EU customers in Singapore, they avoided pretty much all type of regulation. PayPal thwarted capital and qualification requirements by establishing a so called Stored Value Facility, exempt entirely from the requirement of licensing and supervision by the Monetary Authority of Singapore. Nobody is accusing PayPal of being a fraudulent company for this reason as far as I know. So why would New Zealand be any different? Well, it should not be really. It just seems that some bloggers have discovered that Finance Companies from New Zealand have been marketed online to clients worldwide because of the rather attractive legal framework for financial operations involving non-resident clients, and that possibly a minutely small fraction of these companies may have been used for fraudulent activities. Wild accusations targeting pretty much any foreigner setting up a financial company in New Zealand as well as any incorporator assisting with such structuring started to spread across the Net a few years ago. This irresponsible propaganda appeared to have made the Reserve Bank of New Zealand uncomfortable. In response, the Reserve Bank started posting rather odd warning messages online regarding Offshore Finance Companies. The Registry for Financial Service Providers (FSP's) also caught some of the paranoia and started to stall or even stop registrations of Companies with scary foreigners (non-New Zealanders) as directors and/or shareholders. In all fairness, there have been a few rotten eggs among the foreigners setting up New Zealand entities, but in which business sector and in which country do you not get a few rotten eggs? Some Ponzi schemes using New Zealand Finance Companies were discovered back in 2009 or 2010 when such fraudulent operations, sometimes referred to as "mini-Madoffs", were blowing up in different parts of the globe. These cases appear to have been rather limited in scope, especially when compared to the crash and burn of domestic finance companies in New Zealand that have involved very serious fraud and the loss of billions of dollars. These failures had absolutely nothing to do with the offshore sector. Negligent, wreckless and fraudulent New Zealand bankers caused them inflicting enormous losses on New Zealand taxpayers and depositors. This phenomenon seems to have completely and/or conveniently by-passed the attention of these shameless bloggers.

New Zealand remains an attractive jurisdiction for setting up Offshore Finance Companies both for regulatory and tax related reasons, paranoid authorities or not. There are literally hundreds of offshore providers on the Internet offering New Zealand

Finance Company incorporation services and FSP registration. Unfortunately many if not most of them are unable to deliver on half of the promises they make. For some peculiar reason the absolute worst operators never seem to be targeted by the slanderous gossip bloggers.

So why would you want to start your own bank? The reasons vary but many of my clients throughout the past two decades were already managing client funds in one capacity or another when they came to the realization that starting their own bank legally could help them to increase their profits significantly. Fund Managers are often limited to generating revenue from management and performance fees. However, with a banking business they would have the capacity to offer payment services, low or non-interest bearing current accounts, savings accounts and be able to issue certificates of deposit (term deposits). This capacity provides for unparalleled access to low cost money.

If you already have a solid track record for generating respectable investment returns, the switch from a Fund to a Bank can obviously be quite profitable since the Bank would be trading with client funds and not necessarily pass on a substantial share of those profits to the depositors as in the case with a Fund. Other aspiring bankers would consider providing specialized credit. This could entail anything from large project funding to small online payday loans to consumers, or prepaid debit cards and remittance services to "un-bankable" immigrants or people with low credit scores. Some of my clients would set up payroll operations, e-wallets or specialized payment clearing operations, for example secure credit card processing for medium to high risk merchants in specific markets. Others would focus on documentary credit such as letters of credit and financial guarantees for import and export operations. I have helped to establish more than 1000 financial entities through the years and have yet to see two identical business models. The clients would thus typically have a specific niche market in mind. None planned to start their own bank in order to compete with

CITI, HSBC or other banking giants with branches on every corner. I suspect you also have a business model in mind already since you bought this book. I will accordingly not elaborate further on all the possible reasons one could have to start a bank.

The purpose of this book is to provide the reader with the knowledge required to incorporate a New Zealand Company online and to get the same registered as a bona fide Financial Service Provider with the legal capacity to offer banking services to any number of clients resident anywhere in the world. The total investment required for setting up a banking business, just as any other business, obviously varies depending on the business model. It is however quite possible to form and register a legal entity with full legal capacity to offer banking services, for a total cost of less than one thousand dollars, just as the perhaps somewhat controversial subtitle of this book indicates.

One thing that is for certain, after reading this book you will know more about New Zealand Offshore Finance Companies, FSP registration and the regulatory regime in New Zealand than most of the offshore providers I know of who presumably structure such companies for a living. I hope you enjoy reading it, and as always, I welcome feedback and any questions you might have.

Michael Magnusson
readers@michaelmagnusson.com

PART I

The Thousand Dollar Bank

THE LAND WITHOUT A BANKING LAW

New Zealand is a truly unique jurisdiction for international financial activities. My impression is that most New Zealanders are either completely oblivious to this fact or rather disturbed by it if they are aware. The creation of what can in many aspects be considered the least regulated offshore financial center in the world seems to have happened almost by accident. New Zealand used to have a Banking Act but it was repealed in 1995 and replaced with, well, nothing. There are obviously laws in New Zealand regulating financial activities but there are no regulatory entry barriers as such for the business of banking when services are offered to non-residents only (offshore). In the opinion of some people this calls for regulatory change. Some simply accuse anyone in the business of incorporating New Zealand Financial Companies for non-New Zealanders of aiding criminal activity such as international money laundering. The purpose of this book is to provide accurate information about the New Zealand regulatory model from an "offshore perspective". Most parties voicing an opinion on the subject, so far, seem to have been hopelessly misinformed.

I will also describe the process of incorporating New Zealand Companies online and how to register such as Financial Service Providers (FSP's).

New Zealand just as most other countries, has banks operating under supervision by its Central Bank, the Reserve Bank of New Zealand. These companies are referred to as Registered Banks and are subject to strict capital and regulatory requirements just like they would be in any other developed nation. What makes New Zealand unique is that the business of banking is not in any way restricted to these regulated entities. The Registered Banks do not even have a license or permit to engage in the business of banking since such licenses do not exist in New Zealand. This might seem rather controversial or even hard to believe for the uninitiated. I will quote several Reserve Bank articles and documents to clarify this point.

The Reserve Bank of New Zealand summarized the regulatory framework for the New Zealand financial sector in an article prepared in consultation with the Securities Commission and the Ministry of Economic Development:

"Unlike in many countries, where the licensing of a bank determines what the bank can do, bank registration in New Zealand does not determine the permissible activities of a bank. In most respects a Non-Bank Financial Institution can conduct banking business (including deposit-taking and lending on current account) without being a registered bank. Registration as a bank merely enables the entity to include "bank" or a derivative of that word in its name.' (Reserve Bank Bulletin Volume 66, number 4, page 26).

Reserve Bank of New Zealand:

"We do not license the business of banking per se. Financial institutions do not have to be registered banks in order to take deposits and make loans. A financial institution can conduct the business of banking without being subject to the Reserve Bank's prudential requirements for registered banks, so long as it does not use the word "bank" in its name." (Alan Bollard, Reserve Bank

Governor, Financial System Regulation in New Zealand, Financial Sector Ombudsman Conference, 25 July 2003).

Reserve Bank of New Zealand:

"Bank registration does not involve the licensing of the business of banking or deposit taking. It is only if an institution wishes to call itself a bank that there is a requirement for it to be registered by the Reserve Bank of New Zealand. Hence non-licensed institutions are able to take deposits and conduct other aspects of the banking business in New Zealand." (The Role of the Reserve Bank of New Zealand in Supervising the Financial System, RBNZ, March 2001).

Tyree's Banking Law in New Zealand, Second Edition, pages 8-9: "Banking business is not, however, restricted to registered banks. While registered banks' business must comprise of borrowing and lending money and/or the provision of financial services, any non-[registered] bank institution may conduct business that is traditionally regarded as banking business—such as deposit taking, the provision of credit and the offer of cheque accounts and may be regarded as a "banker" for the purposes of mutual common law rights and duties of the banker-customer relationship."

The financial sector in New Zealand has gone through various regulatory changes since these statements were made. I will get in to those changes here, but the statements remain accurate since the business of banking is still not in any way restricted to Registered Banks under Reserve Bank supervision. Nothing has changed in this regard.

If a Company offers banking services and that Company is not a Registered Bank under Reserve Bank supervision, that Company is nevertheless still a Bank from a legal standpoint.

Bills of Exchange Act 1908 (New Zealand) Section 2 Interpretation: A Bank "includes a body of persons, whether incorporated or not, who carry on the business of banking".

There is no statutory definition of "the business of banking" in New Zealand, but the Common Law definition reads as follows:

Business of Banking—means conducting current accounts for customers, where the amounts are repayable to the customer's order, and the person also either collects checks payable to the customer or receives funds from third parties to the customer's current account (Tyree's Banking Law in New Zealand, Second Edition, pages 69-72).

This means that if customers can access their funds held with an institution on demand, and if those customers can either collect checks or receive funds from third parties in their accounts, the entity is indeed a Bank, even if it is not a Registered Bank under Reserve Bank supervision. However, to avoid confusion between a Bank and a Registered Bank, I will use the terms Finance Company or Financial Service Provider hereafter when I refer to a Bank that is not a Registered Bank under the supervision of the Reserve Bank of New Zealand.

Financial Institution means any person including a body of persons whether incorporated or not, who carries on the business of borrowing (deposit taking) and lending money, or providing financial services, or both, as per Section 2 of the Reserve Bank of New Zealand Act 1989.

Deposit taking constitutes an offer of debt securities which is an activity regulated by the Securities Act 1978. The relevant supervisory authority is the Financial Markets Authority (FMA), which was created in 2011 to replace the Securities Commission.

A Finance Company may not issue debt securities to the public in New Zealand without a registered prospectus, a supervisory trustee and the use of investment statements as per the requirements in Part II of the Securities Act 1978. These requirements are however limited to offers of securities to the New Zealand resident public, meaning that an issuer offering securities to non-residents only (offshore) is not captured. Section 7 of the Securities Act 1978:

7. Territorial Scope of Part II:

(1) **Part 2 applies to securities offered to the public in New Zealand**, regardless of-

 (a) where any resulting allotment occurs:

 (b) where the issuer is resident, incorporated, or carries on business.

(2) For the purposes of this Act, a security is offered to a person in New Zealand if an offer of that security for subscription is received by a person in New Zealand, unless the issuer demonstrates that it took all reasonable steps to ensure that members of the public in New Zealand may not accept the offer.

(3) Sections 38B and 58 (except section 58(3) and (4)) also apply to any advertisement that contains or refers to an offer of securities to the public outside New Zealand and that is distributed or to be distributed to a person outside New Zealand by,

 (a) in the case of section 38B, a person resident or having a place of business in New Zealand:

 (b) in the case of section 58, a person resident or having a principal place of business in New Zealand.

(4) For the purpose of subsection (3), the definitions of advertisement and offer extend to communications or offers received by persons outside New Zealand.

(5) The territorial scope of Part 2 may be further extended under Part 5

(6) For the avoidance of doubt, nothing in Part 2 applies to a security or an advertisement unless it applies under subsections (1) to (5).

This section dictates that securities offered by New Zealand issuers to the public outside New Zealand are not captured by the requirements in Part II but criminal liability for untrue statements in advertisements and offers of securities remain.

"Nothing in Part II of the Act applies in respect of any security that is offered for subscription only to persons outside New Zealand and persons in New Zealand who can properly be regarded as having been selected otherwise than as members of the public." Guidebook to New Zealand companies and securities law, 7th Edition, CCH, Andrew Beck and Andrew Borrowdale, page 211.

The Securities Act 1978 consequently does not provide any entry requirements or regulatory hurdles for deposit takers who only offer services to non-New Zealand residents.

Let us then continue to the subject of the Reserve Bank and its licensing regime for non-bank deposit takers introduced in 2008. The regulations require deposit takers to be licensed by the Reserve Bank, to obtain a credit rating and to comply with various requirements with regards to capitalization and governance. These regulations were introduced after some rather substantial failures in the domestic Finance Company sector within New Zealand. The defaulting deposit takers were not related to the offshore industry in any way. They were offering debt securities and loans on the domestic market and their activities were consequently subject to regulation by Part II of the Securities Act 1978 and other legislation. The fact that the necessity for further regulation was triggered by failing domestic deposit takers might explain why the non-bank deposit taking regime adopts the very same geographical scope as Part II of the Securities Act 1978, meaning that offshore deposit taking is not captured by this regulatory framework either. A Deposit Taker as defined in section 157C of the Reserve Bank of New Zealand Act 1989 (as amended at May 1, 2011):

157C—Deposit taker defined

(1) For the purposes of this Part, deposit taker;

(a) means a person who;

(i) **offers debt securities to the public in New Zealand; and**

(ii) carries on the business of borrowing and lending money, or providing financial services, or both

So why does New Zealand so explicitly exclude entities which only offer services offshore from regulation? The main concern of the legislators has obviously been to provide regulatory protection for the resident public. The exclusion of offshore activities must be considered a side effect rather than a result of a deliberate intention to create a virtually unregulated offshore financial center. By capturing offers made to the public in New Zealand "regardless of where the issuer is resident, incorporated, or carries on business", financial entities can effectively be hindered from eluding regulation by offering securities in New Zealand from another jurisdiction, offshore. Anyone making an offer to the public in New Zealand is subject to the regulations, regardless of where the issuer is located which is obviously what the legislators wanted to achieve. The result being that an offer of securities made *from* New Zealand, to customers offshore (non-residents) falls outside the geographical scope of the regulations. Most other jurisdictions regulate offers made "in or from within" their borders and thus capture both domestic and offshore offerings in one sweep. If the legislators in New Zealand had used the words "in or from within New Zealand" instead of "in New Zealand", offshore deposit taking would have become subject to the very same regulation as domestic deposit taking.

Although the deposit taker regulations do not apply to services offered offshore, other parts of the Reserve Bank of New Zealand Act 1989 do apply. Only a registered bank under Reserve Bank supervision is allowed to use the restricted words "Bank, Banker and Banking" in its registered Company name according to provisions in Part 4 of the Act. A non-registered bank can nonetheless use the restricted words in its marketing, subject to disclaimer requirements in accordance with Section 66B:

Limit on use of restricted words in advertisement

(1) No specified person may use a restricted word in any advertisement unless the advertisement contains a statement that complies with subsection (2).

(2) The statement must;

  (a) state that the specified person is not a registered bank; and

  (b) be communicated in a manner that ensures, as far as is reasonably practicable, that the statement attracts the attention of the persons to whom the advertisement is directed.

This means that for example a Finance Company can refer to its services as banking services as long as a disclaimer is included in any marketing material clarifying that the Company is not a

Registered Bank. Disclaimers are often likewise used by Offshore Finance Companies to clarify that services are not available to the public in New Zealand. The following is an example of a suitable disclaimer for a Finance Company using the restricted words in its marketing:

"ABC Finance Ltd is offering financial services as a Finance Company and not as a Registered Bank under Reserve Bank supervision. Services are not available to the public in New Zealand"

The disclaimer must be reasonably visible and attract the attention of potential clients. A disclaimer should not be hidden in the fine print somewhere. I have seen Finance Companies include a disclaimer on their website in such a small font size that one would need a magnifying glass to read it. Such practice would thus constitute a violation of Section 66B, subsection 2B of the Reserve Bank of New Zealand Act 1989.

It took quite some time for the offshore world in general to realize that international banking services could be offered from New Zealand without the extensive entry requirements applicable pretty much anywhere else in the world. Around the year 2008 the offshore players did catch up however and the word spread quickly. Pretty soon an abundance of offers for "Offshore Finance Companies" (OFC's) could be found all over the Internet. This triggered concerns in New Zealand and the Reserve Bank proceeded to put up the following "warning" on its website:

"The Reserve Bank advises that caution should be exercised by anyone considering doing any form of business with entities that promote themselves as "New Zealand offshore finance companies", or use similar descriptions, and that offer financial services either on-line or from locations outside of New Zealand.

No such category of entity is recognised under New Zealand law. The entities involved are usually just registered in New Zealand as companies or limited partnerships, and they have no special status. These entities are not licensed or supervised as financial service providers by any New Zealand authority. They are required to register a New Zealand address, but this is usually that of a compliance agent, with the entities having no real physical presence in New Zealand. These entities are often directed or owned by persons who are not resident in New Zealand. Details about the directors and ownership of these entities can be obtained by searching the on-line database of the New Zealand Companies Office"

So what the Reserve Bank is stating here is that there is no special form of legal entity in New Zealand law called Offshore Finance Company. This should be rather obvious. There is no such thing as a domestic Finance Company defined in New Zealand law either. A Finance Company is simply a company engaging in financial activities. Offshore Finance Company is the term used to describe a Finance Company offering services offshore (to non-residents) only. Naturally a Finance Company would be structured as a regular Limited Company or as a Partnership and so would for example a Car Dealership, Bakery, Book Store, Insurance Company or a Registered Bank under Reserve Bank supervision for that matter. The Reserve Bank goes on by stating that the entities are not licensed or supervised. This is also known and the absence of onerous license requirements was probably one of the main reasons why the OFC's were structured in New Zealand in the first place. Note that the Reserve Bank is not in any way stating that the OFC's should be licensed or supervised. They then go on by stating that many OFC's are owned and operated by foreigners, which is probably also true in many cases.

The only conclusion one can really draw from the rather platitudinous Reserve Bank statement is that it is not too happy about Offshore Finance Companies but it has not found anything legally wrong with them either. Some self-anointed regulatory watchdogs (think bloggers) interpreted the Reserve Bank statement differently however, as if Offshore Finance Companies were somehow illegal. They then proceeded to post their own warnings online about OFC's as well as any company who they became aware of that offered OFC formation services.

I have yet to see anyone, blogger, bureaucrat or otherwise, present any legal argument challenging the legality of the OFC's or the accuracy of claims made by incorporators marketing the same. In all fairness I would agree that it is rather remarkable for a jurisdiction to adopt a regulatory framework that excludes offers of banking services made to non-residents from regulation almost entirely. Pretty much any other jurisdiction would require a full bank license for such activities regardless of where its customers were located. My point is that I fully understand if the New Zealand regulatory model could be perceived as a controversial one. Nonetheless, I find it rather misdirected to blame offshore incorporators for forming companies in accordance with all applicable laws. Unlike in some typical offshore tax haven jurisdictions, the laws in countries like New Zealand are not drafted by offshore service providers (only in our dreams). The simple fact is that the Securities Act 1978 and Deposit Taker regime exclude financial offers made offshore from regulation.

So what happened next? Well, there was a discussion going on for years in New Zealand, long before the non-bank deposit taker regime was introduced, in regards to passing additional legislation regulating the financial services industry. Failing domestic finance companies continued to be a concern of the regulators. That New Zealand was probably one of very few countries in the world having no record of the number of financial institutions operating within its borders was starting to attract international attention. As a result of much discussion and debate the Financial Service Providers (Registration and Dispute Resolution) Act was passed into law in 2008. This led to the opening of a new Financial Service Provider Register (FSPR) in 2010. Any entity or individual who offers any type of financial service from New Zealand is now legally required to register as a Financial Service Provider (FSP). This includes

Registered Banks, Building Societies, Credit Unions, Currency Exchangers, Finance Companies, Payment Processors and so on and also individuals offering financial services or acting as a Financial Advisor. Surely this time the legislators decided to capture services offered offshore? Actually, yes, but not without resistance. The issue here is that with the FSP registration the Offshore Finance Companies (OFC's) would obtain official recognition and increased respectability as financial institutions. Remember the words of the Reserve Bank, "the entities involved are usually just registered in New Zealand as companies or limited partnerships, and they have no special status. These entities are not licensed or supervised as financial service providers by any New Zealand authority". With the new FSP registration in hand the OFC would gain official registration as a financial institution. Since the requirements for registering as an FSP are quite straightforward and involve only a criminal background and bankruptcy check of directors and managers, most OFC's would gladly comply in order to obtain formal registration and recognition as a Financial Institution. Certain parties in New Zealand saw this as a potential problem. The Financial Service Providers (Pre-Implementation Adjustments) Bill, Section 52 reads as follows:

> 52. Not Providing Services in New Zealand. This amendment disqualifies from registration those financial service providers who do not intend to offer services in New Zealand. This should help prevent foreign businesses from setting up 'shell companies' in New Zealand and being able to claim they are regulated under New Zealand law.

The intention before the law was passed was thus to exclude OFC's from the obligation/ability to register as FSP's since they do not provide services in New Zealand.

Shortly after the new Register opened its doors in 2010 some bureaucrat unofficially decided to try and prevent OFC's from complying with the new law and from registering them as FSP's even though section 52 of the Pre-Implementation Bill was specifically rejected by Parliament and no such exclusion provision appears in the final FSP Act. On the contrary, section 8A of the Act clearly specifies that an OFC is indeed required to register:

> 8A Territorial scope
>
> This Act applies to a person who—
>
> (a) **is ordinarily resident in New Zealand** (within the meaning of section 4 of the Crimes Act 1961) **or has a place of business in New Zealand, regardless of where the financial service is provided**; or
>
> (b) is, or is required to be, a licensed provider under a licensing enactment.

Those at the FSPR initially attempted to implement requirements restricting registration only to FSP's that offered financial services from their premises in New Zealand, and making such services available to anyone walking in "off the street". This was clearly absurd given that New Zealand law requires registration "regardless of where the financial service is provided". Such requirement would also indicate that only FSP's providing financial services to retail customers would be required to register, which is clearly not the case. The FSPR agents soon retreated on this requirement and instead started questioning the qualification to register based on subjective interpretations of "ordinarily resident" and "place of business". It was argued that a Company with only a registered office in New Zealand and no further physical presence could not be considered ordinarily resident or to have a place of business there. The New Zealand taxation office among others would on the other hand certainly treat a New Zealand incorporated Company maintaining its registered office in New Zealand as being ordinarily resident. Section 4 of the Crimes Act 1961, which is referred to in the territorial scope of the FSP Act defines ordinarily resident as follows:

> 4. Meaning of ordinarily resident in New Zealand
>
> For the purposes of this Act, a person shall be deemed to be ordinarily resident in New Zealand if;
>
> (a) his home is in New Zealand; or
>
> (b) he is residing in New Zealand with the intention of residing therein indefinitely; or
>
> (c) having resided in New Zealand with the intention of establishing his home therein, or with the intention of residing in New Zealand indefinitely, he is outside New Zealand but has an intention to return to establish his home therein or to reside in New Zealand indefinitely.

A New Zealand Company is by all definitions a New Zealand person and most New Zealand lawyers I have spoken to are of the opinion that its Registered Office can be considered its "home". One or two lawyers found that a Company is ordinarily resident where its management is located. We can however leave the issue of ordinarily resident somewhat open since it is in practice the place of business that has become the main factor for determining whether a Company should register as an FSP.

There is no definition of a "place of business" in any New Zealand law. Nonetheless the FSPR decided in certain cases to demand copies of lease agreements documenting that an FSP applicant was operating from dedicated premises in New Zealand as well as copies of employment contracts evidencing the presence of local staff. Note that there are no such requirements under New Zealand law and again, no actual legal definition of a "place of business" as such exists. Given that FSP registration must precede any FSP activity, it would also be legally impossible for an FSP to start operating and hire staff prior to complying with the registration requirement, creating a catch 22 situation.

Obviously, these erroneous requests for documentation were merely used to discourage "shell companies" from registering as FSP's for the purpose of gaining the added credibility and formal status as registered financial institutions. According to the law anyone offering financial services in or from within New Zealand is required to register as an FSP, whether as a Company or as an individual. Registration is a legal requirement, not a privilege. If you were to offer financial services on the Internet from your Mom's basement in an Auckland suburb, to customers exclusively based in Timbuktu, without leased commercial premises and without employees, you are still required (and should thus be able) to register as an FSP.

The current situation is that the FSPR will stop or delay registration of any entity they consider to not have a place of business of any kind in New Zealand. There are no specific requirements to have employees or dedicated premises, but there should be a proper business address where the Company exercises certain functions. The authorities should be able to make inspection visits at such an address to ensure compliance. It is not possible to register and maintain an FSP on a mere mail drop or virtual office address. I consider this quite a reasonable outcome compared with the initial stance of the FSPR. With a proper place of business and by using the services of local professionals, an FSP can very well offer services to non-residents only, and thus not be subject to regulation of Part II of the Securities Act 1978 or by the Non-Bank Deposit Taker regime, and yet still be registered as a bona fide provider of financial services as required by New Zealand law. This does not mean that the people at the FSPR are all of the sudden happy about offshore entities. They are still on a mission to remove entities from the FSP Register or to stop certain companies they arbitrarily decide they don't like from registering as FSP's, without any valid legal grounds. I will revert to this subject throughout this book.

"Terrible tragedy of the South Seas.
Three million people trapped alive."

Thomas Jefferson Scott

FORCED DEREGISTRATION

Ironically the FSPR appear to have dedicated more tax payer funded resources to blocking FSP's from complying with the law by registering on their Register than they have to their actual mission, which is to enforce the requirement for every single New Zealand Company providing financial services to actually register. So why is the FSPR so determined to stop applicants who pass the criminal background checks and all other requirements of the FSP registration procedure from registering? The explanation is simple. They have concluded that FSP registration provides a certain cosmetic value that they would rather not provide some Offshore Financial Companies with. I say cosmetic value, since the actual qualification requirements for FSP registration are so basic that pretty much anyone 18 years or older would qualify. FSP registration is consequently not in practice an indicator of the level of regulation a registrant is subject to. Those at the FSPR appear to have independently decided that the legal requirements for FSP registration, as per the FSP Act, in their mind are far too relaxed. They seem to be of the opinion that the modern democracy in New Zealand is no longer convenient, that the elected lawmakers indeed got it all wrong, and that surely they know what is best for New Zealand. Hence the FSPR has adopted a whole new role; that of hindering certain applicants from complying with the letter of the law.

The FSP registration might indeed give the impression of the registrant being a regulated New Zealand Financial Institution while in practice its activities can very well be virtually unregulated, especially in cases where services are offered to non-residents only. Although this may be the concern of the FSPR, it does not seem to have been a major concern with the lawmakers. As I mentioned in the previous chapter, the pre-implementation bill which resulted in the Financial Service Provider (Registration & Dispute Resolution) Act 2008 contained a provision restricting registration only to FSP's providing financial services in New Zealand. This provision was clearly rejected by Parliament and the current FSP Act is very clear about the requirement to register regardless of where the financial service is provided.

The geographical scope of the FSP Act which was enacted on September 29, 2008 is clearly defined in Section 8A:

> 8A Territorial scope
>
> This Act applies to a person who—
>
> (a) is ordinarily resident in New Zealand (within the meaning of section 4 of the Crimes Act 1961) or has a place of business in New Zealand, **regardless of where the financial service is provided**; or
>
> (b) is, or is required to be, a licensed provider under a licensing enactment.

Despite the clear geographical scope the FSPR will sometimes ask FSP's to provide documentary evidence of financial services being provided in New Zealand. Some of my clients were threatened with removal from the FSPR in the past based on this invalid argument. Needless to say, an objection to the removal notice was filed clarifying that no requirement exists in New Zealand law for an FSP having to provide services locally in order to be able/required to be registered as an FSP. Although legally obligated to, in my experience the FSPR will often not even respond to legal arguments that they know they cannot challenge. Repeated Official Information Act requests for documentation that evidenced that their stand was legally justified were ignored. In the end local lawyers in New Zealand were forced to bring the matter right up to the Minister of Economic Development (The Companies Office/FSPR operate under this Ministry) who in turn ordered the FSPR to respond. Finally the FSPR's illegal deregistration threats were cancelled. Legal opinions obtained from several prominent New Zealand law firms have confirmed the obvious; FSP registration is required regardless where the financial service is provided. As one Auckland Solicitor stated, "the FSP Act accordingly contemplates that the financial services may be provided outside New Zealand" and "the Registrar would be in breach of its statutory duty if it considered that it was entitled to refuse registration on the ground that the New Zealand entity carries out its services offshore".

In other cases the FSPR have asked applicants to provide evidence of leased commercial premises and local staff. Such requests also lack any legal grounds. I will elaborate on this issue further in the Place of Business chapter.

Entities that have already been registered on the FSPR may be removed from the register if they have not started to offer financial services within three months of having registered as FSP's. This argument for removal is supported by Section 18 (1)(b) of the FSP Act:

18 Deregistration of financial service provider:

(1) The Registrar must deregister a financial service provider after a notice period in accordance with sections 19 and 20, if the Registrar is satisfied that the provider;

(a) is no longer qualified to be registered in accordance with section 13; or

(b) is not in the business of providing a financial service (at any time after the expiry of 3 months after registration); or

(c) has been registered because of a false or misleading representation or omission; or

(d) has proffered an application fee or annual confirmation fee or levy that has subsequently been dishonoured, declined, or reversed.

If the FSPR announce their intention to remove an FSP from the Register based on their assumption that financial services are not being provided after three months or more of having been registered, then either documentary evidence that such services are being provided in the form of accounting records, bank statements, invoices or the like should be provided or the FSP would have to accept deregistration and reregister at a later date when the business is indeed ready to start offering financial services. One always has the right to file an objection when the FSPR announce the intention to deregister an FSP. Although the FSPR seem to continue using arguments known to be invalid to remove entities from the Register, deregistration can and will be stopped if an objection is presented on solid legal grounds. If it cannot be shown that financial services are being offered (in NZ or anywhere else) and three months or more have passed since registration, or if it cannot be demonstrated that a place of business in New Zealand of any kind exists, then deregistration might follow. The process of reregistration would however be required once the circumstances changed.

Another valid reason for removal from the Register would be if misleading information or documentation was provided with the original FSP registration process, see Section 18(1)(c). This provision can be used when removing FSP's which were formed and on sold by questionable offshore service providers registering entities using incorrect or misleading details. However, the most common reason for removal from the FSPR seems to be that the FSPR questions the nature of an FSP's Place of Business, in most cases without any valid legal grounds, by using incorrect arguments that are in direct conflict with the FSP legislation.

It should be noted that if the FSPR wish to remove an FSP from the register based on the alleged absence of a place of business in New Zealand, they are not claiming that the FSP is doing anything illegal by offering financial services to non-residents with a New Zealand entity. They are simply saying that since, in their subjective opinion, the FSP does not have an adequate Place of Business in New Zealand, the FSP Act does not apply and consequently the FSP is not *required* to register. In no way can they order the FSP to seize and desist operations. They, nor anyone else for that matter, can ever accuse an FSP of offering financial services illegally without FSP registration if the FSP was indeed registered (or attempted to register) but the entity was removed from the register or prevented from being registered by the FSPR under the pretext that the entity did not have a sufficient physical presence in New Zealand to trigger the registration requirement. All communications with the FSPR should be kept for the record.

"Never ascribe to malice that which is adequately explained by incompetence."

Napoleon Bonaparte

REGISTERED OFFICE

Every New Zealand Company is legally required to have a physical Registered Office where certain records are maintained and available for inspection. It is absolutely crucial to comply with this requirement. Inspectors from the Companies Office/FSPR often make inspections, especially in cases where entities have foreign directors and/or shareholders and engage in financial activities. Non-compliance with record keeping requirements can lead to substantial fines and in extreme cases the removal of a Company altogether from the Company Register. A Company is further required to have a physical address for service, which can be the same address as the Registered Office. New Zealand Companies are not required to appoint a Resident Agent as are Companies in many other jurisdictions. In practice the provider of the Registered Office, often a local accountancy firm, company formation agent or law firm, performs the functions of a Resident Agent.

The most common Company form in New Zealand is the Limited Company (Ltd), limited by shares of stock. Another entity type gaining increased popularity since its introduction in 2008 is the Limited Partnership (LP). I will provide further details about these entity types in the Company Formation chapter.

A Limited Company is required to maintain up-to-date records at all times at the Registered Office in accordance with of the Companies Act 1993:

Section 186 Registered Office

(1) A company must always have a registered office in New Zealand.

(2) Subject to section 187, the registered office of a company at a particular time is the place that is described as its registered office in the New Zealand register at that time.

(3) The description of the registered office must;

(a) state the address of the registered office; and

(b) if the registered office is at the offices of any firm of chartered accountants, barristers and solicitors, or any other person, state;

(i) that the registered office of the company is at the offices of that firm or person; and

(ii) particulars of the location in any building of those offices; or

(c) if the registered office is not at the offices of any such firm or person but is located in a building occupied by persons other than the company, state particulars of its location in the building.

189 Company Records

(1) Subject to subsection (3) and to section 88 and section 195, a company must keep the following documents at its registered office:

(a) the constitution of the company:

(b) minutes of all meetings and resolutions of shareholders within the last 7 years:

(c) an interests register:

(d) minutes of all meetings and resolutions of directors and directors' committees within the last 7 years:

(e) certificates given by directors under this Act within the last 7 years:

(f) the full names and addresses of the current directors:

(g) copies of all written communications to all shareholders or all holders of the same class of shares during the last 7 years, including annual reports made under section 208:

(h) copies of all financial statements and group financial statements required to be completed by this Act or the Financial Reporting Act 1993 for the last 7 completed accounting periods of the company:

(i) the accounting records required by section 194 for the current accounting period and for the last 7 completed accounting periods of the company:

(j) the share register.

(2) The references in paragraphs (b), (d), (e), and (g) of subsection (1) to 7 years and the references in paragraphs (h) and (i) of that subsection to 7 completed accounting periods include such lesser periods as the Registrar may approve by notice in writing to the company.

(3) The records referred to in paragraphs (a) to (i) of subsection (1) may be kept at a place in New Zealand, notice of which is given to the Registrar in accordance with subsection (4).

(4) If any records are not kept at the registered office of the company, or the place at which they are kept is changed, the company must ensure that within 10 working days of their first being kept elsewhere or moved, as the case may be, notice is given to the Registrar for registration of the places where the records are kept.

(5) If a company fails to comply with subsection (1) or subsection (4),

(a) the company commits an offence and is liable on conviction to the penalty set out in section 373(2):

(b) every director of the company commits an offence and is liable on conviction to the penalty set out in section 374(2).

190 Form of Records

(1) The records of a company must be kept:

(a) in written form; or

(b) in a form or in a manner that allows the documents and information that comprise the records to be easily accessible and convertible into written form.

(2) The board must ensure that adequate measures exist to:

(a) prevent the records being falsified; and

(b) detect any falsification of them.

(3) If the board fails to comply with subsection (2), every director commits an offence and is liable on conviction to the penalty set out in section 374(2).

A Limited Partnership is equally required to maintain a physical Registered Office in New Zealand and to keep records in accordance with Section 74 of the Limited Partnership Act 2008:

74 Records of Limited Partnership

(1) A limited partnership must keep the following records at its registered office:

(a) the partnership agreement and all amendments to it:

(b) minutes of all meetings and resolutions of the partners within the last 7 years:

(c) a list of the names and last known business, residential, or mailing addresses of each current partner and of each person who has ceased to be a partner within the last 7 years:

(d) the capital accounts of each current and former partner for:

(i) the last 7 completed accounting periods of the limited partnership; or

(ii) if 7 completed accounting periods have not elapsed since the limited partnership was first registered, the completed accounting periods since registration:

(e) accounting records that:

(i) correctly record and explain the limited partnership's transactions; and

(ii) at any time enable the financial position of the limited partnership to be determined with reasonable accuracy:

(f) the limited partnership's financial statements prepared in accordance with section 75 for;

(i) the last 7 completed accounting periods of the limited partnership; or

(ii) if 7 completed accounting periods have not elapsed since the limited partnership was first registered, the completed accounting periods since registration.

(2) The references in subsection (1)(b) and (c) to 7 years and the references in subsection (1)(d) and (f) to 7 completed accounting periods include any lesser period that the Registrar may approve by notice in writing to the limited partnership.

(3) The documents in subsection (1) must, subject to the partnership agreement, be available for inspection by any partner during ordinary business hours.

(4) If the limited partnership fails to comply with the requirements of this section;

(a) the limited partnership commits an offence and is liable on summary conviction to a fine not exceeding $10,000; and

(b) each general partner commits an offence and is liable on summary conviction to a fine not exceeding $10,000.

—

As previously mentioned, it is essential that the required records are maintained at the Registered Office at all times. The activity of maintaining these records can also be an important factor for legally establishing the Place of Business, which brings us to the next chapter.

When asked his opinion of New Zealand:
"I find it hard to say, because when I
was there it seemed to be shut."

Sir Clement Freud (Sigmund Freud's grandson)

PLACE OF BUSINESS

We have arrived at the somewhat controversial subject of the New Zealand place of business. The favorite argument of the FSPR in order to try and prevent the compulsory registration of an FSP or to remove an existing FSP from the register is that the entity in question lacks a New Zealand place of business in their subjective view. Note that the FSP Act does not state a *principal* place of business in New Zealand as trigger for the registration requirement, but rather "a" place of business. The Act thus contemplates that a Company can have its principal place of business elsewhere, which of course makes sense considering that non New Zealand Financial Service Providers with a place of business in New Zealand are also required to register with the FSPR, regardlesss of where their principal place of business is located and regardless of in which jurisdiction they were incorporated.

Shortly after the FSPR opened the new register in 2010 they started flagging certain addresses, such as those of known business centers offering virtual office services and known accountancy and law firm offices to prevent registration by applicants located on such locations. I would have gladly accepted it if international clients were exempted from the requirement to register as FSP's based on a provision in the FSP Act dictating that only Companies with employees in New Zealand, or only Companies offering financial services in New Zealand were required to register, but no such provision in law exists. Quite the contrary, as mentioned in previous chapters the New Zealand Parliament specifically rejected Section 52 of the FSP Bill which proposed that only Companies offering financial services in New Zealand should register and they replaced it with a geographical scope capturing all providers of financial services, regardless of where the services are provided.

The FSPR used to disqualify an address as a place of business if they deemed that financial services were not offered to anyone "walking in off the street" at such location. They still appear to do this sometimes. However, the FSP Act is very clear. Any company with a place of business in New Zealand offering financial services anywhere in the world (not necessarily in New Zealand) is required to register with the FSPR. With lack of an exemption by law I could even have considered to accept an official letter from the FSPR confirming that FSP's without employees in New Zealand and which operate through outsourcing agreements with local professionals would be exempt from the requirement to register on the FSPR, but they would of course not provide such a letter. In fact, they are reluctant to communicate any of their reasoning in writing at all and have only provided explanations for stalled applications by phone, totally ignoring requests for clarification sent by email.

So what constitutes a place of business? There is no definition in New Zealand law. So in order to obtain a locally accepted definition, I decided to seek opinions from several prominent attorneys in Auckland. I asked them whether a company without its own dedicated commercial premises or employees, while maintaining a Registered Office in New Zealand and offering services online could somehow be exempt from registering. I knew of course that the FSP Act did not provide for any such exemption but it was time to get something on paper and if those working for the FSPR were not willing to provide it, the law firms would of course be happy to do so, albeit at $500 an hour. These were the exact questions I asked the Auckland solicitors:

1. I need to know if a NZ incorporated Company offering financial services on the Internet from NZ based servers, using a shared business center or secretarial service facility in NZ for its communications would somehow be exempt from having to register as an FSP on the basis of the Company not having a place of business (or insufficient such) in NZ.

2. If so, which type of local physical presence would indeed trigger the registration requirement (type of office space used, number of staff or other parameters)?

   A subsidiary question is:

3. Whether an entity should register as an FSP prior to starting to offer and provide financial services from a place of business in NZ?

I asked the third question for the simple reason that the FSPR had also been known to ask for evidence of financial services being provided by an applicant prior to registration, creating a catch 22 since the FSP Act restricts anyone from providing or purporting to provide financial services without being registered as an FSP.

Not surprisingly, the legal opinions issued in response to these questions were unanimous in regards to the place of business issue; no exemption from the requirement would apply to a company using a shared business center for its business address, engaging secretarial services and offering services online only. The company would be required and should thus be able to register on the FSPR. The distinction between "a" place of business and a "principal place of businсss" was clearly noted and the conclusion was made that a place where the company conduct part of its business, which includes record keeping as prescribed by the Companies Act and other compliance functions, clearly constitutes "a" place of business and in no way would a company be exempt from the obligation to register based on a limited physical presence as described in my first question. Record keeping functions and administration is clearly part of a company's business, as clarified by one solicitor as follows:

"While such activities are clearly an adjunct only to the profit centre, as those same activities are prescribed by statute as mandatory in order for a company to lawfully operate, they also form part of its necessary business".

Another solicitor agreed that a place of business in New Zealand is established if a company carries out part of its business activities there and concluded "it is not necessary for those activities to be a substantial part of the business of the company. It is sufficient if they are incidental to the main activities of the company".

One opinion included further elaboration and references to English court cases that are considered relevant also to New Zealand conditions. In Sabalier vs Trading Co (1927) 1 Ch. 495 at p. 503, it was established that a company which had stopped doing business in England a long time ago maintaining only a registered office at which it performed certain administrative functions, still had a "place of business" in England.

Reference was also made to South India Shipping Corp Ltd vs Export Import Bank of Korea (1985) 2 All ER 219. In this case The English Court of Appeal established that a Bank renting offices in London for administrative functions and from which no banking transactions were performed, indeed maintained a "place of business" in London since the activities were incidental to the main banking activities conducted elsewhere.

As for the timing of FSP registration, the Auckland solicitors also confirmed the obvious; registration must precede the activity and "any advice to the contrary would be foolish and expose the entity to prosecution".

With this legal support from local law firms in hand the FSPR retroceded when objections against deregistration notices were filed on behalf of clients and the place of business issue seemed to have been resolved. Instead the FSPR occasionally started to question whether FSP's were really in the business of providing financial services within three months of having registered. An FSP that has not commenced operations within three months of registering can be removed from the register in accordance with Section 18 (1)(b) of the FSP Act and would have to reregister when the circumstances have changed. This reason for removal is legally grounded and consequently not a point of argument.

I occasionally received emails in the past from people asking me if I could help to stop deregistration of their FSP that they had acquired from some other offshore provider found on the Internet. In some cases they would tell me that their FSP was about to be deregistered due to new regulations in New Zealand requiring local employees and dedicated premises. Apparently many offshore providers have told their FSP clients who receive a deregistration notice for whatever reason, that new regulations were passed in New Zealand requiring a certain minimum physical presence and that this is beyond their control. When people who contacted me confirmed that this was indeed what they had been told, I asked them to request the reference to such regulations from their provider including the date the regulations were passed, what they contain, or anything else evidencing their existence. Their provider could never produce any such reference for obvious reasons. On one occasion one of these unfortunate clients of a competing offshore provider sent me an angry email in which he claimed that he had obtained proof demonstrating that his provider was right after all and I was wrong; that new regulations had indeed been passed requiring employees and dedicated commercial premises for all FSP's. I responded making clear that I was delighted to hear that evidence of these enigmatic regulations had finally been produced and asked him to please forward the same at his earliest convenience.

What came in return was yet another angry email stating that help was no longer required but this time with a forwarded message, purportedly sent by the Companies Office/FSPR with the following content:

"If you wish to maintain the registration as a financial service provider under New Zealand's Financial Service Providers (Registration and Dispute Resolution) Act 2008 you must have a place of business in New Zealand from which you are actually conducting your business. A virtual or serviced office or any other form of contact address from which you are not actually carrying out your business will not be acceptable. The FSP has 20 working days in which to lodge an objection.

Documentation should include:

- *rental/lease agreement*
- *Details of staff employed at this address and how they are providing the financial services*
- *Contact details for the employee or all employees if more than one.*
- *Copies of employment agreements*
- *Job descriptions*
- *Evidence that the employee(s) are NZ citizens, residents or are in NZ on work/study visas etc."*

No references to any section in the FSP Act or to any new regulation was ever provided because again, such does not exist. But at least the FSPR had apparently put their ideas down in writing via an email. I had never seen any of my own clients receive a message of this kind. Note however, that the FSPR were not in any way stating that an FSP without dedicated premises and employees is exempt from registering; they were simply asking for documents which, in their subjective view, would be suitable evidence of a local place of business. No legal grounds for removing an FSP exist based on the absence of dedicated premises or employees. But when the FSPR send a message like the one above it is because they are of some opinion that a particular FSP should not be allowed on their register for whatever reason. If no valid objection were filed, the FSP would indeed be deregistered. The FSPR would certainly never state "absence of employees or absence of lease contract" as a reason for removal. They could only officially state the reason as "not in the business of providing financial services" or similar. The FSPR would probably be able to proceed with removal without resistance since the FSP in question would most likely not even object to the removal notice since the provider that sold the FSP simply blamed new non-existent regulations beyond their control and the client chose to believe this.

I should mention that it is of course entirely possible that the company had not conducted any type of activity at all at its New Zealand address and merely used a secretarial service or mail forwarding facility as address for communications. If no record keeping and similar compliance functions were exercised at the address I would agree that the company could not be considered to have a place of business there. Whatever the circumstances were in this particular case, it was clearly misleading of the FSPR (assuming that the quoted message was actually sent by them) to give the impression that a company without lease contracts or dedicated employees cannot remain on the register of financial service providers. The intention of the law makers was clearly that any provider of financial services should be registered on the FSP register and its principals should pass criminal background checks. To exempt a provider from this requirement based on office space particulars or number of employees would clearly be absurd. Anyone offering a financial service, be they a company or individual, and who has a place of business in New Zealand is required by law to register. A place of business would include a compliance office, a home office or any other place where the company conducts part of its business, with or without employees of its own.

It is obviously the offering of financial services that triggers the registration requirement regardless of the nature or size of an FSP's premises or payroll. If you take a look at the FSP Registration Regulations (included in this book after the FSP Act) it gets even more bizarre. The regulations list the prescribed information that a company is required to provide when registering as an FSP, such as information about financial services to be offered, contact information and so on. Schedule 1, Section 8 of the regulations reads as follows:

A physical address in New Zealand at which the Registrar may contact the applicant (unless the business address provided under section 15(1)(a)(i) of the Act is a physical address in New Zealand).

The regulations consequently contemplate that the place of business address, as prescribed by section 15(1)(a)(i) of the FSP Act, might not even be a physical address in New Zealand, and if this is the case a separate actual physical address must be provided at which the FSPR can contact the company. Silly or not, I would not recommend going in to any elaborate argument with the FSPR about no place of business at all being required in New Zealand as contemplated by these regulations. Sometimes one has to give the dog a bone. However, to accept legally incorrect arguments about FSP's without dedicated lease contracts or employees being unable to register would be giving the dog far too large a bone.

So, we have concluded that if you are planning to set up your own FSP you will need a place of business and it is crucial that you maintain the required records at this address and thus perform some kind of business function from there. You might also want to consider conducting more business from within New Zealand than the bare minimum for compliance purposes. Are you planning to offer credit or debit cards to your customers? Why not mail them from New Zealand? The local postal and courier services work well and rates are reasonable. Local data centers and Internet connections are very reliable thus the IT side of an FSP operation could also be something to consider managing locally.

Perhaps you happen to know someone in New Zealand whom you could ask to provide the address and to keep company records, at least to begin with. A home office can certainly be used as place of business for a smaller FSP operation. The alternative would be to engage a business management firm, accountancy firm or simply to rent and staff office premises. Office space in Auckland and Wellington is readily available at the time of writing and pricing can be quite reasonable when compared to other major cities around the world. You will find plenty of listings by searching for "Auckland Office Space" or similar online. When you call brokers or landlords, be prepared for a rather skeptical attitude. It often feels as though New Zealanders can be rather hesitant and suspicious when approached by someone from outside their two main islands. My impression was always that they look to Australia as a kind of big brother, so when my firm was about to arrange for local office space on behalf of clients I asked a friend in Melbourne to make the calls, since I figured his Aussie accent would not trigger any unnecessary fears of the big unknown. Having spent several hours on the phone with prospective landlords he called me back and said, "I don't know what's going on over there but I am pretty sure DNA testing will be part of their requirements". Apparently most landlords will ask plenty of questions about the anticipated activities of any potential tenant before parting with any details themselves and personal on site interviews would be required. They expected financial details to be provided prior to them parting with any information on their part, as if their office space was the only one on offer in town and one would have to beg for information about the general conditions of a lease. This made it rather difficult to compare the available offers but do not despair, it is certainly possible to rent space in New Zealand. Just be prepared for skepticism, and not only in regards to tenants from off the islands, but also in regards to anything "finance" related.

Remember that domestic finance companies in New Zealand have lost billions due to local fraud and mismanagement. This seems to have caused a general aversion when it comes to this other “f-word”.

"No man is above the law and no man is below it; nor do we ask any man's permission when we ask him to obey it"

Theodore Roosevelt

DISPUTE RESOLUTION SCHEMES

My American clients were sometimes confused by the frequent use of the word "scheme" in New Zealand. In the US one would typically associate the word scheme with a devious or secret plot of some kind, while in New Zealand it is often used to describe a perfectly legitimate plan, project, or program.

I can recall some US clients getting rather offended when New Zealand lawyers and accountants kept referring to their business model as a scheme, which to the clients sounded as bad as if it would have been labeled a scam. So just to clarify, there is nothing devious about a Dispute Resolution Scheme, henceforth DRS.

FSP's that offer services to retail clients are required to join a DRS regardless of whether services are offered to New Zealand residents or offshore only. As the name indicates, a DRS is a facility through which customer disputes can be resolved. Although the FSP is required to have its own internal program for dispute resolution, the DRS provides for additional consumer protection in cases that cannot be resolved internally. There is no cost for the consumer filing a complaint since the DRS are financed entirely by membership fees paid by participating FSP's. If a consumer agrees with the decision issued by a DRS, the decision becomes legally binding for the FSP. Consumers who do not agree with the decision have the option of pursuing other channels, such as the court system and thus disregard the resolution proposed by the DRS. So how can you determine if you are legally required to join a DRS? Some business models are easier to assess than others in this regard, but if your core business is to offer typical retail products to the public you should certainly join a DRS. You may not be required to join a DRS if you only occasionally offer financial services to retail clients providing that such activity does not form part of your principal business. A retail client for DRS purposes is defined as a person who is not a wholesale client, and wholesale clients are typically one of the following:

- Other financial service providers and clients engaging the financial services in the course of their own business, e.g. professional investors

- Large Companies

- Companies associated with the FSP

- Clients receiving a private offer of securities, such as relatives, close business associates, wealthy and sophisticated investors and others who are not considered to be part of the general public as per the Securities Act 1978.

It should be noted that any client can agree to be treated as a wholesale client and thus accept that the FSP is not a member of a DRS. For a detailed definition of a wholesale client please refer to section 49 of the FSP Act (included in this book).

To join a DRS is not a complicated process and membership fees are not excessively high. I therefore see no reason for an FSP to try to avoid this requirement by getting over creative in regards to interpretation of client types. There are currently only three government approved DRS:

Financial Services Complaints Ltd

4th Floor
101 Lambton Quay
Wellington
Postal Address: PO Box 5967 – Wellington 6145
Phone: +64 (0)4 472 3725
Fax: +64 (0)4 472 3728
Web: www.fscl.org.nz
E-mail: info@fscl.org.nz

Insurance & Savings Ombudsman

Level 11
Classic House
15-17 Murphy Street
Wellington 6011
Postal Address: PO Box 10-845—Wellington 6143
Phone: +64 (0)4 499 7612
Fax: +64 (0)4 499 7614
Web: www.iombudsman.org.nz
E-mail: info@iombudsman.org.nz

Financial Dispute Resolution

Level 9
109 Featherston Street
Wellington 6011
Postal Address: P.O. Box 5730—Wellington 6145
Phone: +64 (0)4 910 9952
Fax: +64 (0)4 918 4901
Web: www.fdr.org.nz
E-mail: enquiries@fdr.org.nz

Financial Dispute Resolution (FDR) is the government-established scheme sometimes referred to as the "Reserve Scheme". It seems to be the most straightforward DRS to join. The required membership application forms are available for download on the FDR website. They can be printed, filled out and returned by email or fax. The applicable fees will depend on the volume of your business. Example: If you have less than $1 Million in outstanding loans as a lender you qualify for the lowest fee of NZ$1000 per annum, while up to $200 Million on the books would raise the fee to NZ$5000.

I suggest that you visit the FDR website for complete details about requirements, procedures and costs. It should be noted that the FDR has also issued a guideline document regarding the New Zealand "place of business", from which I quote below:

"Simply providing an address to which correspondence may be delivered would not, of itself, be sufficient. We would expect there to be a physical office, and some people who work there on the company's business. The office need not be the business's principal or sole office. **The business need not be New Zealand based**. A foreign company might legitimately have only a very small office in New Zealand".

"If the people of New Zealand want to be part of our world,
I believe they should hop off their islands, and push 'em closer."

Lewis Black

ONLINE INCORPORATION

The authorities in New Zealand behave in entirely mysterious ways sometimes. They often seem paranoid or terrified of anything "offshore" while at the same time they appear to be incredibly naïve and ignorant when it comes to international compliance. Practically all jurisdictions worldwide, and certainly most typical offshore tax havens, have implemented extensive requirements for identifying beneficial owners and principals of companies and other legal structures for many years. If you have formed a company or opened a bank account anywhere in the world during the last decade or two you will be familiar with these requirements. Companies in most jurisdictions are required to have a locally licensed Resident Agent for record keeping and for the provision of a Registered Office and address for legal service. The agent is normally required to identify all principals of a Company prior to formation and to verify their residential addresses. Some jurisdictions go further by requiring professional references and letters of introduction from any new clients. Any tax haven jurisdiction that does not comply with what have become internationally accepted procedures for client identification and prevention of money laundering would find itself on numerous international black lists. So what about New Zealand? Somehow New Zealand totally missed all these compliance developments worldwide and continued their business as if they had never heard about "Know Your Customer" (KYC) and Anti Money Laundering (AML) measures implemented in nearly every other nation on earth. At the time of writing this book, in early 2013, New Zealand has still not implemented the Anti-Money Laundering and Countering Financing of Terrorism Act that they finally passed in 2009. Imagine a small tax haven country not having an AML Act in force in 2013. The tax haven in question would find itself on every possible blacklist around the world and would be completely slaughtered by the media. There would be accusations of intentional sponsoring of international drug running and terrorism and pretty much every other imaginable evil of the world. There are some reporters and bloggers out there who are so incredibly angry at tax havens that they would not miss such an opportunity. I often wonder if it really is "unfair tax competition" that fuels all this anger towards offshore tax havens. But to sufficiently identify and analyze the real reasons for the aggression would be an entire book of its own. One thing is for certain, a country like New Zealand, which is not generally considered an evil tax haven by the anti-offshore crowd, even though it offers plenty of tax free structures for offshore activities, can get away with extreme blunders when it comes to international compliance and AML. One of these extreme blunders was New Zealand's idea of setting up an online incorporation interface through which anyone, anywhere in the world, could incorporate a New Zealand company almost instantly at a total cost of about $150.00, and with no requirement to identify directors, shareholders or any other party in the process. Any offshore tax haven country even considering setting up such a service would most likely end up with more international sanctions than Iran.

New Zealand eventually woke up and smelled the coffee. But only after a lot of noise had been made. In 2009 a New Zealand Company was incorporated online for the purpose of chartering a Georgian (the former Soviet Republic State, not the US State) registered cargo plane and using it to smuggle 35 tons of illegal weapons from North Korea to Thailand. Later a Justice Ministry Report in New Zealand estimated that New Zealand shell companies were used to launder 1.5 Billion dollars every year. This was all because of the ease at which one could register a New Zealand company online without any identification procedures. Links were found between New Zealand shell companies and the Russian Mafia and Mexico's Sinaloa drug cartel as well as North Korean arms trading. Each time a new scandal blew up in the New Zealand press, the government would send out what seemed to be the same old press release, time after time, announcing that new tough rules would be adopted to stop the abuse.

So what exactly would these tough rules entail? Believe it or not, they are still debating the matter in New Zealand as I write this. The proposed changes initially included some sort of Resident Agent requirement for each company. The government seemed to seriously discuss this issue as if they were about to invent the wheel, and appeared blissfully unaware of the fact that the concept was invented a very long time ago. The final outcome seems to be that all New Zealand Companies will be required to have at least one resident director or a director resident in a trusted non-scary country abroad. So far the only non-scary country that they are considering to grant this trusted status to is, yes you guessed it, their big brother Australia.

Smaller tax haven countries must be observing New Zealand and wonder how on earth a country can get away with all these self-inflicted disasters. As I have already pointed out, any tax haven behaving like this would no doubt be severely punished. New Zealand has so far gotten away with the European Union taking it off the banking and corporate "white list" in mid-2012. Some people in New Zealand perceived this as a major blow. If they only knew how lightly they got away.

Offshore service providers, including my firm, have always identified beneficial owners and principals of companies even though technically this is still not required (as at early 2013) in New Zealand. While the law-makers are lagging behind, the Companies Office have proactively decided to start requesting certified copies of government issued identification and utility bills (as proof of residential address) from directors and shareholders of new companies. Although they forget to ask for identification in some cases, this will become a standard requirement, at least in cases of non-resident directors and shareholders. Note that you can still file for incorporation online. The process has changed only in that the Companies Office will hold your application for incorporation until you provide copies of identification and proof of address.

Another embarrassing blunder by the New Zealand Companies Office was their decision in 2010 to suddenly implement new company name restrictions. This was enforced without any change of legislation, regulation or anything else to support such action. Many companies had been incorporated using the word “Bancorp” or “Bancorporation” in the company name. These names had obviously been duly approved by the Companies Office prior to incorporation. All jurisdictions have clear regulations concerning restricted words that cannot be used in company names. Although amendments can obviously be made to such regulations, I have never seen a Company Registration Authority suddenly invent new restrictions of its own accord forcing existing companies to change names without any legislative grounds to do so. Typically new regulations regarding name restrictions apply only to new incorporations and not to existing companies for what ought to be obvious reasons. However, New Zealand chose to be different than the rest of the world in this regard as well. The Companies Office just decided one day that “Bancorp” and “Bancorporation” were derivatives of the restricted word “Bank” since such words include the word/letters “banc”, which according to the Companies Office translates as “bank” in a foreign language. They did not specify in which language “banc” was supposed to be the word for “bank” nor did they explain why they had approved the allegedly restricted company names in the first place. For example in the US the words “banc” and “bancorp” are often used by banking related (but non-bank) holding entities and subsidiaries. These words are used specifically to avoid the restricted word “bank”.

I find it rather curious that the New Zealand Companies Office did not simply add one letter and pick out the word "banco", which does in fact mean "bank" in Spanish, the second largest language in the world. Anyway, "banc" meaning "bank" or not in some unknown language, the Companies Office ordered every company with an already approved and registered company name containing any of the newly restricted words to change its name immediately, otherwise a forced name change would be performed simply using the company registration number as a new company name. Suffice to say, no company resolution, approval or authorization of any kind by the board of directors or shareholders would be required. The Companies Office would simply edit the entries in the Company Register and change the names, and so they did. Those companies that had not responded to the threat, and thus not voluntarily affected a name change in time, found that their company name had been erased from one day to the next. Their company name had been replaced with simply the company registration number followed by "Limited". I have never seen or heard of such a procedure anywhere else in the world. Not even in cases where companies in fact had the word "bank" in the name and were registered prior to such word becoming restricted.

This is quite controversial if you think about it. A company is a legal person of its own in all aspects of the law and it is identified mainly by its name just like the rest of us. To all of a sudden change its name by force would obviously have serious consequences, especially for a company already doing business all over the world, holding bank accounts, being a party in executed contracts and agreements, owning properties, trademarks and so on.

Many countries also have name restrictions for physical individuals, meaning that parents are not able to give just any name to their children. The main reason for these restrictions is that certain names are considered offensive and may cause suffering to the bearer. Naturally the restrictions are not the same in every country. These restrictions also change from time to time. Imagine if the authorities all of a sudden told you to immediately change your name or they will do it for you, due to new name restrictions that applied retrospectively. Worse still, imagine if you didn't choose a new name for yourself in time, and the authorities simply issued you with a number as your name. The comparison might seem like a bit of a stretch, but it would essentially entail many of the same implications and from a legal point of view it is not a big leap.

So the word "Bank" is a restricted word as well as the word "Bancorp" now. Finance Company names often include words such as "Savings & Loan", "Trust", "Finance", "Financial", "Capital" etc. You can search for availability of your prospective company name on companies.govt.nz.

Let us move on to the actual procedure of incorporating a New Zealand company online.

Start by going to companies.govt.nz and:

1. Click on "Register".

2. Click on "Create your RealMe (formerly known as igovt) login now".

3. Provide your email address and choose a username and password. The New Zealand phone number is not mandatory.

4. Choose three security questions and provide answers. This information is requested if you ever forget your password

5. Accept the terms and conditions by ticking the box at the bottom of the screen.

6. Enter the letters in the security image and click "Create my RealMe login".

You now have a RealMe account that can be used for access to various government websites. Let us continue by creating a Companies Office user account:

1. Click on "Return to Companies Office".

2. Choose account type, individual or organization. An individual account is the most suitable for most users and can also be used to manage multiple companies.

3. Enter name and address. If you are using a non NZ address, click on "Manual or Overseas", enter the address and then click on "Use this address". Click on Continue.

4. Enter a phone number and a mailing address (if different from the physical address provided in the previous step), tick the box for accepting the terms and conditions. Click on Register.

5. You have the option to setup a direct debit arrangement for payment of registry fees. This only works when using a NZ bank account. If you do not have a NZ bank account, tick the box for "No" and click Continue. You will be able to pay fees using a credit or debit card issued in any country.

6. Done! You now have a Companies Office user account linked to your RealMe account. You will now be redirected to the incorporation interface. If the signup process is interrupted prior to completion for any reason, just log in with your RealMe credentials at companies.govt.nz. The process will then be resumed and you will be able to provide any missing information.

So let's incorporate, shall we? If you have been logged out, just log back in at companies.govt.nz to get to the main user dashboard. The first thing you need to do is to reserve a company name for your new entity.

1. Click on "Reserve a Company Name" in the left hand side menu.

2. Enter the proposed company name ending with the word "Limited" (do not use the abbreviation Ltd at this point) and confirm.

3. Confirm acceptance of the fee (NZ$ 10.22) and click on Payment.

4. Enter debit/credit card information and click Submit. You will receive an invoice by email.

Company name approval will typically be obtained within one hour or less during New Zealand business hours. You will be notified by email once the name has been approved. After receiving approval, log back in at companies.govt.nz and:

5. Click on "Start a Company"

6. Click on "Incorporate a NZ Company"

7. Choose your already approved name in the popup window and click on continue.

8. Enter number of directors, shareholders and shares. You need a minimum of one director and one shareholder (can be the same person). Directors must be physical individuals while shareholders can be either individuals or legal entities. Both Directors and shareholders can be of any nationality and resident anywhere in the world. You can

have any amount of shares, but a common number would be 100 or 1000. I suggest that you un-tick the box for tax registration. You can register for tax any time. Click on Next Step, Company Addresses.

9. Leave the option regarding management by business professional un-ticked unless your company will be managed by a law firm, accountancy firm or the like.

   Enter your New Zealand physical address to be used as registered office. If the complete address does not show up in the automated search, click on "enter address manually".

   Address for service can be and usually is the same as registered office, but if you prefer you can choose an alternative address for legal service and for communications.

   Enter the company email address and phone numbers (phone and fax are optional).

   Choose filing month for annual return/company renewal. This has nothing to do with tax return filing. It is simply the month in which you will be requested to reconfirm the company details each year starting the year after incorporation.

   Address for share register is optional. You should only provide an address here if your share registers will not be kept at the registered office.

   Click on: Next Step, Directors.

10. Enter each director's first and last names complete and exactly as they appear in their passport or other government issued identification. Do not use initials. Be sure to use the director's complete physical residential address. Foreign

directors will be asked for a certified copy of identification as well as a recent utility bill, so the address provided here must match the utility bill. Further contact information is optional. Click on: Next Step, Shareholders.

11. Choose Shareholders from the Directors and/or provide new shareholders. Click on: Next Step, Share Allocations.

12. Enter share allocations. If you have only one shareholder, enter the total number of shares next to the name of the shareholder. Click on: Next Step, Constitution.

13 A constitution is optional and essentially sets out the rights, powers and duties of the company, the board and each director and shareholder. If a company is incorporated without a constitution, its internal procedures are automatically governed by the Companies Act 1993. It can be helpful to have a constitution since banks and other third parties outside New Zealand often expect to see more company documents than just a certificate of incorporation and registry extract. Third parties might be used to seeing a 'Memorandum and Articles of Association' or similar documentation used in other jurisdictions. The constitution will serve the same purpose as those documents. You can purchase and use a standard constitution from the Auckland District Law Society, www.adsl.org.nz or CCH, www.cchforms.co.nz, or you can proceed without a constitution.

14. Choose "I don't want to apply for a company IRD number (Tax ID) at this time.". I suggest registering for tax later and to engage a NZ accountant for advice in regards to reporting requirements and tax liability. Click on: Next Step, GST Registration.

15. GST (sales tax) registration is not possible if you chose to not apply for an IRD number in the previous stage. The

GST number can also be obtained later by you or your accountant. Click on: Next Step, Review.

16. Review your details and correct any errors if needed. Proceed to payment of the incorporation fee, $150,00 in total. You will receive an invoice by email after completed payment.

17. Submit your application by clicking on "Incorporate".

18. You will receive consent forms by email. The forms need to be signed by the director(s) and shareholder(s) and returned by fax in accordance with the instructions on the form, or scanned and uploaded though the online user interface.

This used to be the end of the procedure. After uploading or faxing the consent forms in step 18 you would typically receive the certificate of incorporation and company registry extract by email within minutes and your company would be ready. As I mentioned earlier in this chapter, the Companies Office have adopted certain identification requirements after realizing that an anonymous company formation and registration procedure was not such a great idea after all. So instead of receiving an email confirming your incorporation you are now more likely to receive a message asking for the following documents from each director and shareholder:

- The signed consent form in original
- Certified Copy of passport
- Certified Copy of recent utility bill (not older than 3 months)

If you do not have a passport, two pieces of other government issued identification will also be accepted, such as Social Security Certificate and Driver's License. Copies should be certified by lawyer, notary or Justice of the Peace and include full contact details as well as the wording "True Certified Copy of the Original" or similar.

As previously mentioned, directors and shareholders can be of any nationality and can be resident anywhere in the world. You might nevertheless want to consider partnering up with or hiring someone in New Zealand who can act as a director. Your company will be met with less skepticism in New Zealand if you have a local director onboard. And besides, regulations will soon be introduced which will require a local director.

A local director can also be helpful when establishing a place of business for FSP purposes. When the FSPR tries on their invalid argument that only companies with dedicated premises and locally hired staff can be registered as FSP's, remember such erroneous claims can quite easily be fought with proper legal arguments, which this book provides you with. Having said that, it is more challenging to demonstrate that a Company has local operations if it only has foreign directors and shareholders and no principals in New Zealand, whether as management or on staff. Since a New Zealand (or Australian) director will soon be required for compliance purposes anyway, and a local director can very well manage the local FSP place of business and provide the address for such, the benefits of having a local partner are accordingly numerous. In today's world of social and business networking online you should not find it too difficult to come across a prospective partner or employee in New Zealand. You could also consider advertising in local newspapers or on local web sites such as hotfrog.co.nz and trademe.co.nz.

You might also benefit from having a local shareholder, whether an individual or another legal entity. It is common to use an offshore holding company as sole shareholder but by doing so you trigger requirements to present audited financial statements to the Companies Office every year (see companies.govt.nz for further details about financial reporting requirements and other ongoing obligations).

There are also potential tax consequences to consider. You can only have physical individuals as shareholders if you wish to qualify for the relatively new "Look Through Company" (LTC) regime, which can provide for total tax freedom in entities with foreign source income and non-resident shareholders. See the "New Zealand as a Tax Haven" chapter for further information.

When George Bernard Shaw visited New Zealand, a reporter asked him his impression of the place and after a pause, Shaw replied: "Altogether too many sheep."

LIMITED PARTNERSHIP FORMATION

The Companies Office have been promulgating for several years that it will soon be possible to register a Limited Partnership (LP) online. They have yet to deliver on that promise as I write this book. Currently the only way to get an LP registered is by sending in physical paper forms. Nor are you able to find an existing LP in the regular company name search online. You must go to companies.govt.nz, click on "Online Services" and "Search Other Registries" in the menu. You will then be taken to a separate search interface where you can tick the box for LP's and enter the relevant keywords. People trying to verify an LP online, such as a bank employee considering a new bank account application, commonly miss the somewhat obscure search function and thus conclude that the company in question cannot be found in the New Zealand Company Register. This is one of the minor disadvantages associated with an LP. Another is the meager company documentation provided by the Registrar. While properly designed Certificates of Incorporation and Company Register Extracts can be downloaded anytime for regular Limited Companies, an LP is provided with a miserable looking Certificate of Registration by snail mail upon registration. The certificate often looks like it has been sent through a chain of five or more fax machines before reaching your mailbox. This often prompts banks and others who might need to review your corporate documentation to question where the original Certificate of Registration is. Ordering a certified copy of the Certificate of Registration from the Companies Office can solve this issue. The Certificate will still look as though it has been faxed around a few times but an original certification will be attached to it. Another factor to consider is that although the LP has gained popularity during the past few years, the regular Limited Company legal form is the most widely recognized.

So what are the advantages of an LP? There are actually several benefits and they will likely compensate quite well for the disadvantages. The LP is a "pass through" vehicle, meaning that the LP itself is not assessed for tax. The partners are responsible for any applicable taxation on their share of any profit. Non-resident partners can qualify to reap the benefits of New Zealand's various double taxation agreements. Offshore partners may not even be taxed on their foreign source income depending on the rules in the home jurisdiction. Regular Limited Companies can also be treated as a "pass through" under the recently introduced Look Through Company regime but only if they have physical individuals (maximum of 5) or trustees as shareholders. The LP has no such restrictions so partners can be either legal entities or physical individuals from any country.

Privacy can be another benefit of an LP. Information regarding General Partners, who are responsible for all debts and liabilities of the LP, is publicly available in the LP Register. Information regarding Limited Partners, who are only responsible for their capital investment in the LP, is treated as confidential and not publicly available.

You can find further information about the LP regime at this web address:

http://www.business.govt.nz/companies/learn-about/
other-entities/limited-partnerships

The registration form is very straightforward and simply needs to be filled out with the proposed name of the LP, its registered address in New Zealand and the names and addresses of the General and Limited Partners (minimum of one each). The registration form can be downloaded here:

http://www.business.govt.nz/companies/pdf-library/forms/limited-partnership-forms/form-lp1-pdf

Each general partner also needs to sign a consent form which can be downloaded here:

http://www.business.govt.nz/companies/pdf-library/forms/limited-partnership-forms/form-lp5-pdf

The proposed partners must certify that they have entered into a partnership agreement compliant with section 10 of the Limited Partnerships Act 2008. A local lawyer can draft a partnership agreement or a compliant template can be purchased here:

http://www.zealandfinancial.co.nz/nz-limited-partnership

The government registration fee for a New Zealand LP is NZ$270.00 which can be paid by check or credit card.

"The government solution to a problem is usually as bad as the problem."

Milton Friedman

FSP REGISTRATION

We have reached the crucial step of getting your Limited Company or Limited Partnership registered as a bona fide provider of financial services in accordance with the Financial Service Provider (Registration & Dispute Resolution) Act 2008. The FSP Act dictates that any individual or legal entity offering financial services and that is ordinarily resident or has a place of business in New Zealand, is required to register as an FSP regardless of where the financial services are provided.

Entities that need to register as FSP's include Banks, Brokers, Credit Unions, Finance Companies, Investment Advisors and Insurers, to mention a few examples.

1. Go to fspr.govt.nz and click on "log on". Enter with your RealMe credentials.

2. Click on "Register an FSP" in the left hand side menu.

3. Click on "NZ Registered Entity"

4. Enter the beginning of your company name in the search field and locate the company.

   Add additional trading names if applicable.

Enter your "place of business" address or tick the box for "Same as Registered Office".

Enter email address.

Choose filing month (the month you will be asked to reconfirm FSP details annually)

Click on "Proceed to Financial Services"

5. Choose the financial services the FSP will be offering. Please note that you should not choose services that you do not intend on providing. You should consider whether registering for a particular service could trigger additional regulatory requirements, such as licensing requirements. For example, if you intend the FSP to take deposits exclusively from non-residents you should not tick the "Deposit Taker" box, since a Deposit Taker is defined as a person offering debt securities to the public in New Zealand (see Chapter 1). An FSP can legally take deposits from the public offshore and operate outside this definition. If you tick the box for Deposit Taker you will hear from the Reserve Bank, since you have then in effect stated that you will be taking deposits from the resident public in New Zealand. As another example, ticking the box for "Insurer" would not make your company an insurance company. You cannot offer insurance services without triggering additional regulatory requirements. The following services do not in themselves trigger additional license requirements and are often chosen by Offshore FSP's:

    - Keeping, investing and managing money, securities and investment portfolios on behalf of third parties.

    - Providing credit under a credit contract (lending)

- Operating a money or value transfer service
- Issuing and managing means of payment
- Giving financial guarantees
- Changing foreign currency
- Entering into or trading on an exchange, in an over-the-counter market or otherwise, the following on behalf of another person:
    - money market instruments (including cheques, bills, certificates of deposits);
    - foreign exchange (including forward foreign exchange contracts);
    - derivative products including, but not limited to, futures and options;
    - exchange rate and interest rate instruments, including products such as swaps and forward rule agreements;
    - transferable securities;
    - other negotiable instruments and financial assets

These services would typically cover the range of activities which most offshore FSP's would engage in, such as deposit taking (offshore), investment management, payment services, card issuing, issuing of financial guarantees and foreign exchange services. I would also suggest that you seek local legal advice in regards to the specific services you are planning to offer in order to fully assess your regulatory obligations.

Indicate whether you are offering services to retail clients for DRS purposes. If yes, indicate which DRS your FSP is a member of.

Click on "Proceed to Directors"

6. Enter Gender and Date of Birth of the Director(s).

   Click on "Proceed to Controlling Owners"

7. Identify any individuals or entities that own more than 50% of the FSP shares, if applicable.

   Click on "Proceed to Senior Managers".

8. Identify any Senior Managers, if applicable. This step is not mandatory. A Senior Manager means a person who is not a director but holds a position that gives him/her significant influence over the management or administration of the FSP, for example a chief financial officer.

   Click on "Proceed to Review"

9. Review and submit your application or make changes if required. All directors, controlling owners and senior managers will be background checked. This entails a search of criminal history and bankruptcy records in New Zealand.

The fees payable for FSP registration and annual returns are currently as follows:

FSP Registration:	NZ$ 357.78
Financial Markets Authority (FMA) Levy:	NZ$ 350.00
Criminal Background Check (per person):	NZ$ 40.25
DRS Verification:	NZ$ 30.67
Annual Return:	NZ$ 61.33

"We contend that for a nation to try to tax itself into prosperity is like a man standing in a bucket and trying to lift himself up by the handle."

Winston Churchill

NEW ZEALAND AS A TAX HAVEN

Most of the members of the anti-offshore crowd seem to be ignorant of the fact that New Zealand is quite a prominent offshore tax haven offering excellent zero tax structures. As a party to 37 international double taxation agreements, New Zealand is generally perceived as a high tax country and thus usually not a target in the international campaign against tax havens. One of the most popular offshore structures in New Zealand is the Offshore Trust, or Foreign Trust, which allows for a high level of privacy and absolute tax freedom. A foreign trust is one with a non-resident settlor and non-resident beneficiaries but with at least one local trustee, which can be an individual or a legal entity, for example a Limited Company or Partnership. The New Zealand foreign trust is one of the most attractive asset protection and tax avoidance vehicles available today, especially considering the increasingly hostile attitude towards more traditional tax havens worldwide.

The tax-free trust regime has not eluded criticism entirely however. In a TV interview on New Zealand's TV3 edition of 60 Minutes which aired on September 7 2012, Revenue Minister Peter Dunne was asked critical questions around the foreign trust concept. The local Green Party found the interview upsetting and immediately prepared a press release in which they criticized the trust regime as well as Dunne's defense of the same. I quote from the Press Release:

"Revenue Minister Peter Dunne tonight endorsed tax avoidance as a legitimate practice when challenged about the use of secret New Zealand foreign trusts as a tax haven.

TV3's 60 minutes highlighted problems with the trusts and Mr. Dunne responded that the behaviour was "legitimate tax avoidance".

Mr. Dunne's repeated reference to legitimate tax avoidance was astounding. The tax system is being undermined by the minister in charge of it," Green Party co-leader Russel Norman said."

It seems as if Green Party co-leader Russel Norman may have overlooked the fact that tax avoidance in most forms is indeed legitimate and legal, as opposed to tax evasion.

The media release continued:

> *"New Zealand's foreign trust law allows non-residents to set up trusts here in New Zealand holding assets not liable for taxation. There are approximately 8000 foreign trusts registered with the Inland Revenue Department (IRD) holding assets estimated to be worth tens of billions of dollars. Little information is required to register a foreign trust which means ownership is effectively anonymous and assets are invisible.*
>
> *"New Zealand's foreign trusts hide billions of dollars of assets and should be broken open to help stop the global tax evasion industry," said Dr. Norman."*

The Limited Partnership (LP) introduced in 2008 provides for another potentially tax free New Zealand structure. The LP is tax transparent, meaning that income passes through it without any tax assessment. The partners can be offshore entities or non-resident individuals who are not subject to taxation on their foreign source income in their country of tax residence. Information about general partners, who are responsible for all debts and liabilities of the LP, is publicly available in the LP register while the identities of the limited partners, who are only responsible for their capital investment, is treated as confidential.

If this would not be enough to make New Zealand qualify as a proper tax haven, the Look Through Company (LTC) tax regime for Limited Companies introduced in 2011 should seal the deal. A LTC must comply with the following:

1. Have 5 or fewer shareholders

2. Be New Zealand resident for tax purposes

3. Issue only shares that have the same voting and participation rights

4. Have only natural persons or trustees as shareholders

The LTC is fiscally transparent and thus identical in its tax treatment to a Limited Partnership. Section BD 1(5)(c) of the Income Tax Act 2007 further provides an exemption from tax in New Zealand on income derived by a non-resident provided that income does not have its source in New Zealand. This means that a foreign shareholder of a LTC that only receives offshore income will not be subject to any tax in New Zealand.

Did I mention that there is no general capital gains tax in New Zealand nor any inheritance or estate taxes?

While some features of the regulatory framework for offshore banking activities may have been conceived by accident, New Zealand's tax haven aspirations are clearly anything but accidental. Having said that, the government will of course quickly deny that any such aspirations exist or ever existed.

Let us move on to a tax issue more specific to offshore banking. A New Zealand entity paying interest to non-residents is required to withhold 15% of the interest paid as Non-Resident Withholding Tax (NRWT). The NRWT applies to any type of interest or dividend payments made to clients offshore and consequently include interest payments on bank deposits. However, do not despair; New Zealand came up with a creative solution here as well. You simply need to register as an Approved Issuer under the Approved Issuer Levy (AIL) regime and register each interest bearing debt security for AIL. As an Approved Issuer you are allowed to pay interest to non-residents at zero rate of NRWT and instead pay a 2% levy on the amount paid. You are not required to report the identity or location of the customers you are paying interest to. You simply report monthly how much interest you have paid to non-residents, and pay 2% of the total as AIL.

You can access full details about AIL at the following URL:

http://www.ird.govt.nz/nrwt/approved-issuer-levy/

You can register as an Approved Issuer online or by filling out form IR396. You need to register each debt security, meaning each interest bearing account type that you offer to your non-resident clients. This would include for example interest bearing savings accounts, term deposits and bonds. You can register each security by using form IR397. The IRD site contains all the relevant forms for downloading and a wealth of information on this subject. You might also want to download the AIL Guide, IR395.

Before you can apply for AIL your company needs to have an IRD number (Tax ID), which you can obtain by filling out form IR596.

You can also register for Goods and Services Tax (GST) online on the IRD website. GST is the equivalent of sales tax or Value Added Tax (VAT) in other countries. In principle you are required to register for GST if you carry out taxable activity and your turnover was over $60,000 during the past 12 months, or is expected to be so for the next 12 months. Financial Services are however generally exempt from GST. Search on "GST and financial services" on the IRD website for further details.

I strongly recommend that you engage the services of a Chartered Accountant in New Zealand in order to properly assess your tax liabilities and in order to identify any benefits and exemptions for which you may qualify depending on the nature of your anticipated activities.

"Liberty consists in the power of doing that which is permitted by the law."

Marcus Tullius Cicero

ANTI-MONEY LAUNDERING & KNOW YOUR CUSTOMER

New Zealand was a true latecomer in passing proper Anti-Money Laundering legislation. Although they finally passed the Anti-Money Laundering and Countering Financing of Terrorism Act (AML Act) in 2009, this legislation does not fully come in to force until June 30, 2013. Prior to the AML Act customer identification and suspicious transaction reporting was regulated by the Financial Transactions Reporting Act 1996. This act simply dictates that financial institutions should take "reasonable measures" to verify the identity of their customers. The AML Act dictates procedures more in line with internationally accepted standards.

In order to comply with the AML Act you will be required to have the following:

- A Risk Assessment of the money laundering and financing of terrorism that you could expect in the course of running your business

- An AML/CFT Program that includes procedures to detect, deter, manage and mitigate money laundering and the financing of terrorism

- A Compliance Officer appointed to administer and maintain your AML/CFT program
- Customer Due Diligence processes including customer identification and verification of identity
- Suspicious Transaction Reporting, Auditing and Annual Reporting systems and processes

The requirements are very similar to what you would see in any other internationally compliant jurisdiction. The main difference is that the authorities in New Zealand have actually done an absolutely excellent job when it comes to facilitating compliance with the Act. In most other countries you would be expected and required to develop compliance manuals, AML programs, customer identification procedures and so on. The authorities would rarely provide any documentation other than the AML Act itself. It could easily cost tens of thousands of dollars in fees to lawyers and other compliance professionals when developing AML/KYC manuals and other documentation. Not only would you be required by law to have such documentation in place, banks and other counter parties will often ask about your AML program and KYC procedures when you apply to open a new account.

The authorities in New Zealand have prepared an impressive range of documentation that can save you a lot of time and money. The Codes of Practice and Guidelines which can be downloaded from the Department of Internal Affairs website, make the development of any internal compliance documentation very straightforward given that all the hard work and expense has pretty much been performed already.

The following guideline documents are crucial and extremely helpful for AML and KYC purposes:

- Beneficial Ownership Guideline
- Guideline for Audits of Risk Assessments and AML/CFT
- Countries Assessment Guideline
- AML/CFT Program Guideline
- In the Ordinary Course of Business Guideline
- Identity Verification Code of Practice 2011
- Risk Assessment Guideline

The guides describe in detail how you are expected to identify various types of customers such as Companies, Individuals, Partnerships, and Trusts. It further describes acceptable types of identification and proper certification of photocopies. All these guideline documents can be downloaded in Word or PDF format on the following page:

http://www.dia.govt.nz/diawebsite.nsf/wpg_URL/Services-Anti-Money-Laundering-Codes-of-Practice-and-Guidelines

The guides are practically turnkey compliance programs. By copying the well-defined procedures from the various guides you will have no problem to develop your own internal AML and KYC documentation and with so much comprehensive documentation readily available free of charge, there is no excuse for non-compliance.

*“Whenever a man does a thoroughly stupid thing,
it is always from the noblest of motives”*

Oscar Wilde

WHAT HAPPENS NEXT?

There have been some further developments in New Zealand worth mentioning while I have been writing the previous chapters of this book. The FSPR are still unhappy about offshore FSP's potentially using the register for what they perceive to be mainly cosmetic purposes. They have started to send out responses like the one below when they receive applications that they deem require further scrutiny:

> *"Dear Sir*
>
> *I refer to your query regarding the application to register ABC Finance Ltd Limited as a financial service provider.*
>
> *The Financial Markets Authority and the Registrar have formed the view that "place of business" for the purpose of the Financial Service Providers (Registration and Dispute Resolution) Act 2008 ("the FSP Act") requires the company to have a physical presence at an address in New Zealand from which the financial services are provided. The Registrar and/or the FMA need to be able to visit the business address and make enquiries of management of*

the company or its employees in the event that a complaint is received.

For the purposes of enforcement of the registration requirements under the FSP Act, we consider it relevant to consider where a company's business is being transacted from and by whom in this country. We do not consider that mere incorporation in New Zealand, or the existence of a registered office address here (under the Companies Act 1993), is in itself evidence that a company has a place of business in New Zealand.

The FMA has supported the position taken by the Registrar that a "place of business" in New Zealand is not established by simply being a New Zealand incorporated company and having a virtual office or using the address of a third party (such as an accountant or law firm) in New Zealand. We have been advised that the FMA is also of the view that the financial services business must be carried on in New Zealand, although the recipients of the services may be offshore. The FMA considers this approach is consistent with the legislative purpose in section 9 of the FSP Act, in particular, to establish a compulsory public register to enable regulation of financial service providers, to prohibit certain people from being involved with financial service providers and to conform with New Zealand's obligations under FATF.

If you wish to proceed with the application to register ABC Finance Limited as a FSP, you will need to provide information (including supporting documentation) as to how ABC Finance Limited will be transacting its business from 555 ABC Street and how it will be providing its financial services from this address.

If this company is providing online financial services and does not have a business address in New Zealand from which it is transacting its business, it is not required to register as a financial service provider."

The messages seem to vary somewhat depending on who the applicant is. In some cases the FSPR appear to have included more specific instructions, such as: "You have to rent an office in New Zealand in order to register". In other messages they ask for employee contracts, job descriptions, and details about operating hours at the place of business and detailed descriptions of the financial services to be offered. Several Offshore Service Providers on the Internet have been totally mislead by this and have even copied and pasted the message from the FSPR on to their websites, referring to the same as "new legislation". The people at the FSPR must be laughing out loud on their coffee breaks. So for the sake of clarity, no new legislation has been passed relating to this issue, and no changes have been made to the geographical scope of the FSP Act. As a matter of fact, the proposition of making changes in regards to the place of business requirement and geographical scope has been specifically rejected, yet again. I will come back to that in a moment.

So why am I so focused on this place of business issue? Pretty much all other countries require a physical presence of some kind for a banking operation after all. Indeed they do, but they typically have very clear qualification criteria and their regulators, at least in civilized countries, can be expected to abide by applicable laws. If authorities discover that a law is flawed, they should seek to have that law amended. I detest public servants who decide to intentionally abuse their positions of servant-hood to promulgate false information suiting their own private agendas in clear violation of the laws that it is their duty to uphold and to enforce. I have seen plenty of government abuse throughout my career. It is common that authorities in third world countries more often than not ignore their own laws entirely. It seems as if some countries have laws in place merely for cosmetic purposes. Government abuse and corruption should not be tolerated under any circumstances.

In the case of New Zealand and the FSPR, giving them the benefit of the doubt, even if we assume that the authorities are acting with good intentions, that still does not justify flagrant abuse. While the FSPR might intend to stop illegitimate operators from registering in New Zealand, which of course is a noble motive, they effectively sabotage applications from pretty much any entity with a non-New Zealand director or shareholder onboard even if the applications fulfill every requirement prescribed by the FSP Act.

The people at the FSPR have on occasions been known to question the viability of proposed financial services to be offered by an FSP, even though they are not qualified nor authorized to make such assessments. Questions about operating hours and job descriptions have no bearing on the obligation to register as an FSP. I would strongly recommend the people at the FSPR to read their own job descriptions before asking for those of others. The FSP registration procedure should be dictated by objective qualification criteria rather than subjective guesswork and fantasy requirements created out of thin air by registry clerks and other bureaucrats as they see fit.

While the people at the FSPR pretend as though changes were made to the FSP Act already, and most Offshore Service Providers have been fooled into believing them, there are in fact some real changes in the pipeline. I quote from a rather interesting government document below:

"This Regulatory Impact Statement has been prepared by the Ministry of Business, Innovation and Employment.

It provides an analysis of options to minimize misuse of the Financial Service Providers Register by overseas based financial service providers in order to ensure that New Zealand remains a trusted place to do business. The status quo is not considered to sufficiently enable the Registrar of Financial Service Providers and the Financial Markets Authority to prevent the registration of financial service providers with no substantive link to New Zealand."

I shall continue with their definition of the problem at hand:

"Status quo and problem definition

1. *The Financial Service Provider (Registration & Dispute Resolution) Act 2008 (the FSPA), was part of financial sector reforms in 2008 that aimed to promote confidence in financial markets. The FSPA established a public register for all financial service providers (FSP's). The purposes of the registration system are to prevent certain people from providing financial services in New Zealand; assist regulators with the regulation of the financial sector; and to ensure that consumers have access to free dispute resolution services. The FSPA applies to FSP's that are ordinarily resident in New Zealand or have a place of business in New Zealand, regardless of where the financial service is provided.*

2. *Since the registration regime came into effect in 2010 a significant number of offshore based FSP's have sought to register in New Zealand, in order to take advantage of New Zealand's reputation as a well regulated jurisdiction."*

Here the document starts looking like it has been sanitized by the CIA or Pentagon. Many sections have been blacked out, or "redacted" and the ministry supports this censorship with several articles of the Official Information Act 1982, among them section 9(2)(g)(i) which reads as follows:

9 (2) Subject to sections 6, 7, 10, and 18, this section applies if, and only if, the withholding of the information is necessary to;

(g)(i) the free and frank expression of opinions by or between or to Ministers of the Crown or members of an organisation or officers and employees of any department or organisation in the course of their duty.

The Official Information Act 1982 is meant to ensure that the public has access to official information, but it thus also includes provisions for quite the opposite, namely for government officials to censor information so that frank opinions can be exchanged in the course of their duty, without public knowledge of what is being done and said. They left enough information in order to determine where things are heading however. The document describes three different possible solutions to the "status quo":

"Option 1: Changes to Scope and Registration Criteria

The territorial scope of the FSPA and the qualifications for registration could be amended to clearly exclude either FSP's that do not offer a financial service from New Zealand or FSP's that do not have a substantive presence in New Zealand. Changes to the territorial scope of the Act and/or the registration criteria could provide both the Registrar and applicants with clear criteria regarding which FSP's are not able to register in New Zealand. This would provide for an efficient registration process and would minimize the impact of this problem on the Registrar and FMA's resources.

However, any relatively minor changes to the geographical scope and/or the registration criteria are unlikely to be effective in preventing misuse of the register, as offshore based FSP's are likely to adjust their operations to meet the amended requirements. On the other hand, significant changes to these criteria run the risk of having significant unintended consequences. Adopting a narrower definition of "place of business", for example, could allow some actual New Zealand-based FSP's to avoid registration by ensuring that they do not have a "place of business" that meets that requirement. We consider that it is important that the FSPA remains comprehensive in its coverage of New Zealand-based FSP's"

There we go. At least the people behind this document seem to understand that it would be absurd to implement requirements of dedicated staff or office space, since an FSP with a shared office or operated by its owners or contracted professionals rather than by employees, would then be exempt from registration, criminal background checks etc. The FSPR obviously pretend as if Option 1 has already been decided upon and that such "proposed" changes to the FSP Act have already been passed into law. Several Offshore Service Providers have simply decided to believe the same. The reality is that Option 1 has been rejected by the government.

"Option 2: Licensing of Services

The offshore-based FSP's that are of concern are attempting to register for financial services which do not require licensing in New Zealand. A number of other jurisdictions license all financial services. In Australia, for example, all entities that provide financial services are required to obtain an Australian Financial Service License, which involve demonstrating to the regulator that they are competent and sufficiently resourced to carry on the proposed business. The licensing process allows the regulator to impose a range of requirements on applicants and ensures that all Australian FSP's, including those that are based offshore, are appropriately regulated.

However, it would disproportionate to license all New Zealand FSP's. We are of the view that for a number of classes of financial services the costs on providers would outweigh the benefits of a licensing system. The costs associated with even a relatively light 'fit and proper' licensing system for all FSP's would be significant and would only be justified if there were a broader public benefit in imposing further requirements. These costs would include an expansion of the FMA's licensing processes and systems and both direct and indirect costs on FSP's associated with the licensing process and ongoing regulatory requirements."

So, the option of implementing new licensing and qualification requirements is dismissed mainly because the costs engendered are believed to outweigh the possible benefits. I certainly agree that it would be disproportionate to change the entire regulatory system for financial services in an attempt to discourage some offshore operators from registering on the FSP register. This takes us to option 3, which has been partially censored, but the point is clearly made:

"Option 3: Changes to Registrar's powers and disqualification criteria (Preferred option)

13. *We recommend introducing three measures to directly target the identified problems, without significantly impacting on the wider group of legitimate FSP's.*

    Allowing the FMA to decline registration or de-register FSP.

14. *This amendment would give the FMA the power to direct the Registrar to decline a registration (in case of new applications), or to de-register an FSP (in the case of registered FSP's) where the FMA is not satisfied that registration is necessary or desirable in light of the purpose of the FSPA.*

Withheld under s9(2)(g)(i) of the Official Information Act 1982

16. *The proposed powers would allow the Registrar to refer clearly suspicious applications, and existing FSP's about which it has concerns, to the FMA for further consideration. The FMA is well placed to make determinations of this matter due to due to its*

role as the supervisor of financial markets participants. The FMA would consider a number of matters in deciding whether to decline registration or to de-register an existing FSP, in light of the purposes of the Act. We anticipate that this will include assessing whether the FSP actually intends to offer services from New Zealand or to New Zealanders. The purposes of the registration part of the FSPA include enabling the Registrar and other regulators to regulate financial service providers and to conform with New Zealand's obligations under the Financial Task Force recommendations.

17. *The power would allow the FMA to look at the substance, rather than the form, of the FSP's operations. If, after examining the details of a FSP's operation, the FMA is confident that it is not desirable or necessary for the FSP to be registered, it will direct the Registrar to decline registration or de-register the FSP. If it is not clear that a new application is genuine, the applicant will likely be registered, although their operations might be monitored to see whether they qualify for further registration".*

The third option is what has been deemed the most viable route to take and the Cabinet has approved these measures. The Cabinet paper can be found here (follow the FSP changes link):

http://www.med.govt.nz/business/business-law/current-business-law-work/

So what does this mean in practice? Well, I believe there are both positive and negative aspects to consider. The FSPR will simply keep sniffing out new applications and existing FSP's that they deem require further scrutiny. A positive development is that it will be the people at the FMA, not the FSPR, looking at any "suspicious" applications and deciding whether an entity should be registered as an FSP or not. The FSPR have not proven to be good at playing financial regulators and should not be asking questions when they are highly unlikely to understand the answers. The FMA, the legitimate financial regulator, should indeed have staff qualified to handle these matters. The efficiency of these new measures will be assessed in a statutory review of the FSP regime in August 2015. Until then, further changes are unlikely.

Again, to date no changes have been made to the geographical scope or place of business requirements. When applying for FSP registration, simply be prepared to present documentation, preferably a business plan describing the services to be offered, the background of the principals and other basic information about the anticipated operation. Whether you are or plan to lease your own dedicated office space or use a serviced office center or some other arrangement, be sure to include documentation. If you do not have your own employees, include copies of contracts documenting how the company will be operated using business management professionals or the like.

Since there is not and will not be any clear definition of a "place of business", you basically just have to convince the FMA that your business is not a scam and that the company has or will have some kind of local operation. This should not really be considered a hurdle for anyone with a legitimate business concept. Please also note that it is stated in the Regulatory Impact document that "If it is not clear that a new application is genuine, the applicant will likely be registered, although their operations might be monitored to see whether they qualify for further registration". This indicates a more reasonable and professional handling than the FSPR approach, which at times consisted of simply trying to stop all applications that they did not like, period.

If the FMA tell the FSPR to turn down your application, they would most likely do so with the justification that you do not need to be registered as an FSP, since in their view you do not operate from New Zealand. Note the FSPR message in the beginning of this chapter: "If this company is providing online financial services and does not have a business address in New Zealand from which it is transacting its business, it is not required to register as a financial service provider." You could thus still offer financial services, but without requirement to be registered on the FSP Register. The authorities can never accuse you of illegally offering or purporting to offer financial services with a New Zealand Company without FSP registration if they are the ones stating that you are not required to have such registration. You would then simply operate as an Offshore Finance Company, rather than as a registered FSP.

Therefore, the efforts of the authorities in New Zealand to prevent illegitimate offshore operators are almost completely misdirected. They are simply looking in all the wrong places when trying to find a solution. They have entirely missed the point that New Zealand was already a jurisdiction of choice for Offshore Finance Companies long before the FSP Register was introduced. Sure, the Offshore Finance Companies decided to register as FSP's when such registration became available, since the law said that they should, and indeed, this registration potentially provided them with additional credibility as financial institutions. The main reason why offshore operators from all over the world choose New Zealand was never the FSP registration however, added cosmetic value or not. They choose New Zealand because there are no entry barriers for the business of banking there. A New Zealand company can take deposits, make loans and offer other financial services to any number of clients all over the world (except the public in New Zealand) without being subject to any capital requirements, qualification requirements or other regulatory hurdles. This makes New Zealand unique, and we can keep discussing the particulars of whether a company with or without a broom closet in New Zealand should register as an FSP, but the fact remains, offers of financial services to non-residents are not subject to the regulatory requirements set out in Part II of the Securities Act 1978, nor the requirements for Deposit Takers under supervision by the Reserve Bank. So the stand made by the FSPR regarding registration does absolutely nothing to curb the activities of Offshore Finance Companies. A rogue operator will continue to escape all the safeguards built into the registration process and now do so with the blessing of the FMA and FSPR.

There are some important regulatory changes on the way that are worth mentioning here. Although the "issues" with Offshore Finance Companies do not seem to have played a major role in the drafting of the Financial Markets Conduct Act that was passed on September 13, 2013, this new law will indeed subject most such entities to additional regulation. Several but not all parts of the Act will apply to entities offering securities exclusively to non-residents. One example is Part 4 which contains requirements for a prospectus, supervisory trustee and other provisions with regards to governance. These requirements will take effect on December 1, 2014. A two-year transition period will give Finance Companies until December 1, 2016 to comply. Exemptions apply for entities offering services exclusively to wholesale or wealthy customers and for private offers of securities.

In my opinion, the most efficient solution to discourage dishonest operators from establishing offshore deposit taking entities would be to simply change the scope of the deposit taker regime. However the Reserve Bank does not seem to consider fraudulent offshore deposit takers to be a major issue, thus no such change is currently being considered. In a report from September 2013 on the operation of the prudential regime for Non-Bank Deposit Takers, the Reserve Bank makes the following statement (Section 146):

"We think that entities that are funded through offshore sources should generally not come within the scope of the definition. This is because we think that the risk to the New Zealand financial system from the failure of this kind of entity is generally less than would be caused by the failure of a domestically funded entity."

If all deposit taking, whether from New Zealand residents or from offshore, were subject to the capital adequacy, credit rating and qualification criteria dictated by the Reserve Bank, New Zealand would no longer be the country where you can set up a Bank with a thousand dollars, or with even less if you can legally avoid FSP registration. That is after all what currently makes New Zealand, the land without a banking law, unique in the world.

FEEDBACK

Questions?

Comments?

Please Share!

readers@michaelmagnusson.com

Follow Michael Magnusson on Twitter for Offshore Banking and Tax Haven News:

@magnussonwrites

BIBLIOGRAPHY

The source material used for Part I includes but is not limited to the following:

New Zealand Legislation (available at legislation.govt.nz):

Anti-Money Laundering and Countering Financing of Terrorism Act 2009

Banking Act Repeal Act 1995

Bills of Exchange Act 1908

Companies Act 1993

Crimes Act 1961

Financial Markets Authority Act 2011

Financial Markets Conduct Act 2013

Financial Reporting Act 1993

Financial Service Provider (Dispute Resolution and Registration) Act 2008

Financial Service Provider (Registration) Regulations 2010

Financial Service Providers (Pre-Implementation Adjustments) Bill

Financial Transactions Reporting Act 1996

Limited Partnership Act 2008

Reserve Bank of New Zealand Act 1989

Securities Act 1978

Reserve Bank Bulletin Volume 66, Number 4
www.rbnz.govt.nz/research/bulletin/2002_2006/dec2003.html

Alan Bollard, Reserve Bank Governor, Financial System Regulation in New Zealand, Speech at the Financial Sector Ombudsman Conference, 25 July 2003
www.rbnz.govt.nz/research/search/article.asp?id=3766

The Role of the Reserve Bank of New Zealand in Supervising the Financial System, RBNZ, March 2001
www.rbnz.govt.nz/finstab/banking/role_financialsys.pdf

Tyree's Banking Law in New Zealand, Second Edition
Authors: Alan L Tyree, Caroline Kidd, Charles Rickett and Duncan Webb
ISBN: 9780408715089

Guidebook to New Zealand companies and securities law
CCH, 7th Edition
Authors: Andrew Beck and Andrew Borrowdale

Financial Dispute Resolution Membership Application
www.fdr.org.nz

Approved Issuer Levy Guide IR395
www.ird.govt.nz

Financial Intelligence Unit, New Zealand Police
National Risk Assessment 2010
http://www.justice.govt.nz/policy/criminal-justice/aml-cft/publications-and-consultation/national-risk-assessment-2010

Strengthening New Zealand's Resistance to Organised Crime An all-of-Government Response – August 2011
http://www.justice.govt.nz/publications/global-publications/s/strengthening-new-zealands-resistance-to-organised-crime

Regulatory Impact Statement prepared by the Ministry of Business, Innovation and Employment, Undated
http://www.med.govt.nz/business/business-law/current-business-law-work/financial-service-provider-registration-changes/FSPA-registration-amendments-RIS.pdf

Financial Service Provider Registration Amendments
Office of the Minister of Commerce, Undated
http://www.med.govt.nz/business/business-law/current-business-law-work/financial-service-provider-registration-changes

Review of the Prudential Regime for Non-Bank Deposit Takers
Reserve Bank of New Zealand - September 2013
http://www.rbnz.govt.nz/regulation_and_supervision/non-bank_deposit_takers/5475890.pdf

"Laws are like sausages, it is better not to see them being made."

Otto von Bismarck

PART II

Legislation

FSP (Registration & Dispute Resolution) Act 2008

FSP (Registration) Regulations 2010

Financial Service Providers (Registration and Dispute Resolution) Act 2008

Reprinted as at 1 October 2011

Public Act 2008 No 97
Date of assent 29 September 2008
Commencement see section 2

Contents

Part 3

Dispute resolution

49E Giving revocation of certification or notification of opt out
49F Members of dispute resolution scheme must comply with rules and binding resolutions
49G Offence to fail to comply with District Court order
50 Meaning of approved dispute resolution scheme
51 Application for approval
52 Mandatory considerations for approval
53 Minister must decide application for approval
54 Notification and publication of decision
55 Reapplication by unsuccessful applicant
56 Withdrawal of approval
57 Notice of intention to withdraw approval
58 Objection to intended withdrawal of approval 46
59 Approval is withdrawn from date person responsible for scheme is notified
60 Notification and publication of withdrawal of approval
61 Effect of withdrawal of approval on members of dispute resolution scheme
62 List of members
63 Rules about approved dispute resolution scheme
64 Obligation to publish rules
65 Duty to notify change to rules
66 Minister's consideration of change of rules
67 Duty to co-operate and communicate information in certain circumstances
68 Annual report
69 Person responsible for approved dispute resolution scheme must supply further information on Minister's request
70 Annual report and information requested by Minister to be publicly available
71 Reserve scheme
72 Appointment of reserve scheme
72A Reserve scheme: rules about fees and charges
73 Revocation of appointment as reserve scheme
74 Notice of intention to recommend revocation of appointment as reserve scheme under section 73(2)(a) or (b)

Schedule 1
Consequential amendment

Schedule 2
Licensing authorities and licensed providers

---

1 Title

This Act is the Financial Service Providers (Registration and Dispute Resolution) Act 2008.

2 Commencement

(1) Part 2 and section 48 come into force on a date to be appointed by the Governor-General by Order in Council; and 1 or more orders may be made that do either or both of the following:

(a) bring different provisions into force on different dates:

(b) bring provisions into force on different dates in respect of different types of financial service or financial service provider.

(2) The rest of this Act comes into force on the day after the date on which it receives the Royal assent.

Part 1
Preliminary provisions

3 Overview

(1) This Act requires financial service providers to be registered.

(2) In order to be registered, financial service providers are generally required to be members of a dispute resolution scheme if they provide financial services to retail clients.

(3) The Act sets out how a dispute resolution scheme may be approved by the Minister, why the approval might be withdrawn, and how a dispute resolution scheme may be appointed as the reserve scheme.

(4) The Act provides that the reserve scheme is to act as the default dispute resolution scheme and is to be capable of resolving disputes relating to all types of financial service providers.

(5) This section is intended as a guide only.

4 Interpretation

In this Act, unless the context otherwise requires,-

affiliated entity means an affiliated entity that has been identified in an Order in Council in accordance with section 23(3)

annual confirmation means the annual confirmation relating to a registered provider supplied to the Registrar under section 28.

annual report means the annual report relating to an approved dispute resolution scheme supplied to the Minister under section 68

approved dispute resolution scheme has the meaning given by section 50

broker has the meaning given by section 77A of the Financial Advisers Act 2008

broking service has the meaning given by section 77B of the Financial Advisers Act 2008

business includes any profession, trade, or undertaking, whether or not carried on with the intention of making a pecuniary profit

chartered accountant has the same meaning as in section 2 of the Institute of Chartered Accountants of New Zealand Act 1996

chief executive means the chief executive of the department of State that, with the authority of the Prime Minister, is for the time being responsible for the administration of this Act

company means a company, or an overseas company, within the meaning of section 2(1) of the Companies Act 1993

contract of insurance-

(a) means every contract of insurance including a contract of life insurance (including endowment and annuity contracts) and reinsurance; but

(b) does not include a class of contract declared not to be a contract of insurance by regulations

controlling owner means, in relation to a financial service provider that is not an individual, any person who beneficially owns 50% or more of that provider

conveyancing practitioner has the meaning given by section 6 of the Lawyers and Conveyancers Act 2006

credit contract-

(a) has the meaning given by section 7 of the Credit Contracts and Consumer Finance Act 2003; but

(b) does not include-

(i) contracts specified in section 15(1)(a) or (b) of that Act:

(ii) contracts to be treated as credit sales and consumer credit contracts under section 16 of that Act:

(iii) contracts under which no interest charges as defined in section 5 of that Act are payable

director has the meaning given by section 126 of the Companies Act 1993, but also includes, in relation to a body that is not a company, a person who occupies a position comparable to that of a director (such as a trustee or a partner)

document means-

(a) any material, whether or not it is signed or otherwise authenticated, that bears symbols (including words and figures), images, or sounds, or from which symbols, images, or sounds can be derived, and includes:

(i) a label, marking, or other writing that identifies or describes a thing of which it forms a part, or to which it is attached:

(ii) a book, map, plan, graph, or drawing:

(iii) a photograph, film, or negative; and

(b) information electronically recorded or stored, and information derived from that information due date, in relation to an annual confirmation, means the date allocated to a registered financial service provider by the Registrar under section 16(1)(b)

family trust has the same meaning as in section 5 of the Credit Contracts and Consumer Finance Act 2003

FATF means the Financial Action Task Force on Money Laundering established in Paris in 1989

FATF Recommendations means all of the following recommendations:

(a) the 40 Recommendations adopted by FATF at its plenary meeting on 20 June 2003:

(b) the Special Recommendations on Terrorist Financing adopted by FATF at its extraordinary plenary meeting on 31 October 2001:

(c) Special Recommendation IX on Terrorist Financing adopted by FATF at its plenary meeting between 20 and 22 October 2004

financial adviser service has the meaning given by section 9 of the Financial Advisers Act 2008

financial service has the meaning given by section 5

financial service provider means a person who provides or offers to provide a financial service

in the business of providing a financial service has the meaning given by section 6

incorporated law firm has the meaning given by section 6 of the Lawyers and Conveyancers Act 2006

insurer means a person by whom or on whose behalf the risk or part of the risk to which any contract of insurance relates is accepted

lawyer has the meaning given by section 6 of the Lawyers and Conveyancers Act 2006

licensed means licensed, registered, authorised, or otherwise approved by a licensing authority

licensed provider means a person, identified in Schedule 2, who-

(a) provides or offers to provide a licensed service; and

(b) is licensed, registered, authorised, or otherwise approved by a licensing authority

licensed service means a financial service in respect of which a licensing enactment requires a person to be licensed (or to be exempt from that requirement) to-

(a) provide the service; or

(b) hold out that the person provides the service

licensing authority means a body, identified in Schedule 2, that licenses, registers, authorises, or otherwise approves a person to be a licensed provider

licensing enactment means an enactment identified in Schedule 2 **member**, in relation to a dispute resolution scheme, has the meaning given by section 48(2)

member of a local authority has the meaning given by section 5(1) of the Local Government Act 2002

Minister means-

(a) the Minister of the Crown who, under the authority of any warrant or with the authority of the Prime Minister,is for the time being responsible for the administration of this Act and for Parts 1 and 2; and

(b) the Minister of the Crown who, under the authority of any warrant or with the authority of the Prime Minister, is for the time being responsible for Part 3

Ministry means the department of State that, with the authority of the Prime Minister, is for the time being responsible for the administration of this Act

person includes a corporation sole, a body corporate, and an unincorporated body prescribed means prescribed by this Act or by any regulations made under this Act

real estate agent means a person who is a licensee under the Real Estate Agents Act 2008

register means the register of financial service providers established and maintained under section 24

Registrar means the Registrar of Financial Service Providers appointed under section 35

related company has the meaning given by section 2(3) of the Companies Act 1993

reserve scheme has the meaning given by section 71

responsible financial service provider is a person declared to be a responsible financial service provider under section 23(1)

retail client has the meaning set out in section 49

senior manager means, in relation to a financial service provider, a person who is not a director but occupies a position that allows the person to exercise significant influence over the management or administration of that provider (for example, a chief executive or a chief financial officer) tax agent has the meaning given by section 3(1) of the Tax Administration Act 1994

wholesale client has the meaning set out in section 49.

5 Meaning of financial service

In this Act, financial service means any of the following financial services:

(a) a financial adviser service:

(ab)a broking service:

(b) acting as a deposit taker as defined in the Reserve Bank of New Zealand Act 1989:

(c) being a registered bank:

(d) keeping, investing, administering, or managing money, securities, or investment portfolios on behalf of other persons:

(e) providing credit under a credit contract:

(f) operating a money or value transfer service:

(g) issuing and managing means of payment (for example, credit and debit cards, cheques, travellers' cheques, money orders, bankers' drafts, and electronic money):

(h) giving financial guarantees:

(i) participating in an offer of securities to the public in either of the following capacities (within the meaning of those terms under section 2(1) of the Securities Act 1978):

  (i) as an issuer of the securities:

  (ii) as a promoter:

(ia) acting in any of the following capacities (within the meaning of those terms under section 2(1) of the Securities Act 1978) in respect of securities offered to the public:

  (i) as a trustee:

  (ia) as a statutory supervisor:

  (ii) as a unit trustee:

  (iii) as a superannuation trustee:

  (iv) as a manager:

(j) changing foreign currency:

(k) entering into derivative transactions, or trading in money market instruments, foreign exchange, interest rate and index instruments, transferable securities (including shares), and futures contracts on behalf of another person:

(l) providing forward foreign exchange contracts:

(m) acting as an insurer:

(n) providing any other financial service that is prescribed for the purposes of New Zealand complying with the FATF Recommendations, other recommendations by FATF, or other similar international obligations that are consistent with the purpose of this Act.

6 Meaning of in the business of providing a financial service

In this Act, in the business of providing a financial service means carrying on a business of providing or offering to provide a financial service (whether or not the business is the provider's only business or the provider's principal business).

7 Application of Act

(1) This Act applies to persons who are in the business of providing a financial service.

(2) None of the following persons are in the business of providing a financial service for the purposes of this Act to the extent this subsection applies to them:

(a) a lawyer, incorporated law firm, conveyancing practitioner, chartered accountant, tax agent, or real estate agent providing a service in the ordinary course of business of the relevant kind:

(b) a government department listed in Schedule 1 of the State Sector Act 1988:

(c) the Reserve Bank of New Zealand (and any subsidiaries):

(d) the statutory entities listed in Schedule 1 of the Crown Entities Act 2004:

(e) a person engaged in terminating the business of a financial service provider after that provider has been deregistered:

(f) a non-profit organisation in respect of free financial services:

(g) an affiliated entity:

(h) an executor, administrator, or trustee in respect of services provided in the administration of an estate or a trustee in respect of services provided to beneficiaries of a family trust:

(i) a nominated representative (within the meaning of the Financial Advisers Act 2008) while acting in that capacity:

(j) an employer while providing services to enable employees of the employer to obtain rights or benefits under a registered superannuation scheme (as defined in section 2(1) of the Superannuation Schemes Act 1989) or a KiwiSaver scheme (as defined in section 4(1) of the KiwiSaver Act 2006), being a scheme in which that employer participates for the benefit of its employees:

(k) any person exempted, under regulations made under this Act or by or under any other enactment, from the application of this Act or from the requirement to register under this Act (to the extent of the relevant exemption).

(3) If subsection (2) applies to a person (A), it applies equally to any controlling owner, director, employee, agent, or other person while acting in the course of, and for the purposes of, A's business to the same extent as it applies to A.

(4) However, subsections (2) and (3) do not apply if, and to the extent that, any other enactment requires a person referred to in those subsections to be registered under this Act.

8 Act binds the Crown

This Act binds the Crown.

8A Territorial scope

This Act applies to a person who—

(a) is ordinarily resident in New Zealand (within the meaning of section 4 of the Crimes Act 1961) or has a place of business in New Zealand, regardless of where the financial service is provided; or

(b) is, or is required to be, a licensed provider under a licensing enactment.

Part 2
Registration

9 Purpose of this Part

The purpose of this Part is to—

(a) establish a compulsory public register of financial service providers to enable—

(i) the public to access information about financial service providers; and

(ii) the Registrar and other regulators to regulate financial service providers:

(b) prohibit certain people from being involved in the management or direction of registered financial service providers:

(c) conform with New Zealand's obligations under the FATF Recommendations.

10 Registration and deregistration

(1) Registration under this Act continues until the registered person is deregistered.

(2) Registration may not be transferred and may not vest by operation of law in any person other than the person registered under this Act.

(3) A person is deregistered when the Registrar enters on the register that the person is deregistered.

11 No being in business of providing financial service unless registered

(1) A person to whom this Act applies must not be in the business of providing a financial service unless that person is registered for that service under this Part.

(2) Every person who knowingly breaches subsection (1) commits an offence and is liable on summary conviction,—

(a) in the case of an individual, to imprisonment for a term not exceeding 12 months or to a fine not exceeding $100,000, or to both; or

(b) in the case of a person who is not an individual, to a fine not exceeding $300,000.

12 No holding out that in business of providing financial service unless registered

(1) A person to whom this Act applies must not—

(a) hold out that the person is registered under this Act unless that person is registered under this Part; or

(b) hold out that the person is registered in respect of a particular service or entitled, qualified, able, or willing to be in the business of providing a financial service unless that person is registered for that service under this Part.

(2) Every person who knowingly breaches subsection (1) commits an offence and is liable on summary conviction,—

(a) in the case of an individual, to imprisonment for a term not exceeding 12 months or to a fine not exceeding $100,000, or to both; or

(b) in the case of a person who is not an individual, to a fine not exceeding $300,000.

13 Qualifications for registration as financial service provider

A person is qualified to be registered as a financial service provider if—

(a) the person is not disqualified under section 14; and

(b) the person is a member of an approved dispute resolution scheme, or the reserve scheme, if required by section 48; and

(c) if a licensing enactment requires the person to be a licensed provider, the person is, or will be (on and from commencing to be in the relevant business), a licensed provider.

14 Disqualified person

(1) A person is disqualified if,—

(a) in the case of an individual, the individual is disqualified under subsection (2); or

(b) in the case of a person who is not an individual, the person has a controlling owner, director, or senior manager who is disqualified under subsection (2).

(2) The following persons are disqualified:

(a) an undischarged bankrupt:

(b) a person prohibited from being a director or promoter of, or concerned in the management of, an incorporated or unincorporated body under the Companies Act 1993, the Securities Act 1978, the Securities Markets Act 1988, or the Takeovers Act 1993:

(c) a person subject to a management banning order under the Securities Act 1978, the Securities Markets Act 1988, the Takeovers Act 1993, or subject to an order under section 108 of the Credit Contracts and Consumer Finance Act 2003:

(d) a person who has been convicted of an offence against section 11, 12, or 41 within the past 5 years:

(e) a person who has been convicted of an offence under sections 217 to 266 of the Crimes Act 1961 within the past 5 years:

(f) a person who has been convicted of a money laundering offence or an offence relating to the financing of terrorism:

(g) a person who is subject to a confiscation order under the Proceeds of Crime Act 1991.

(3) A member of a local authority must be treated as if he or she is not disqualified.

15 Application to be registered as financial service provider

(1) An application to be registered as a financial service provider must be made to the Registrar and—

(a) state the following (as relevant to the applicant):

(i) the name and business address of the applicant:

(ii) the name and business address of the approved dispute resolution scheme or the reserve scheme of which the applicant is a member:

(iii) whether the application relates to a licensed service, and if so, which particular licensed service; and

(b) be in the form (if any) required by the Registrar; and

(c) confirm that the applicant is not disqualified under section 14; and

(d) contain, or be accompanied by, any other prescribed information or documents; and

(e) be accompanied by the prescribed fee or levy (if any).

(2) If the application relates to a licensed service, it must be accompanied by any information required, by or under the licensing enactment, to become a licensed provider.

16 Registration of financial service provider

(1) If the Registrar accepts that an applicant is qualified to be registered as a financial service provider, the Registrar must—

(a) enter the following details on the register (as relevant to the provider):

(i) the name and business address of the provider:

(ii) the name and business address of the approved dispute resolution scheme or the reserve scheme of which the provider is a member:

(iia) the type or types of financial service for which the provider is registered:

(iii) if the provider is a licensed provider in relation to a particular licensed service, that fact and the name and business address of the relevant licensing authority:

(iv) any other information prescribed in regulations; and

(b) allocate a due date for the provider's annual confirmation, notify the provider of that date, and notify that date on the register.

(2) If the Registrar does not accept that an applicant is qualified to be registered as a financial service provider, the Registrar must notify the applicant and any relevant licensing authority of the Registrar's decision.

17 Duty to notify changes relating to financial service provider

(1) Each of the following persons must notify the Registrar about the following relevant changes relating to a financial service provider:

(a) a financial service provider, if—

(i) the provider knows that the provider is no longer qualified for registration in accordance with section 13; or

(ii) the provider is in a business of providing a financial service for which the provider is not registered; or

(iii) the provider knows that any details on the register are no longer correct:

(b) the licensing authority, if the licensing authority knows that a financial service provider has ceased to be licensed:

(c) the person responsible for an approved dispute resolution scheme or the reserve scheme of which a financial service provider was a member, if the person knows that the provider is no longer a member of that scheme.

(2) The time within which a person must notify the Registrar under subsection (1) is 10 working days from the date the person comes to know about the change.

(3) A financial service provider who breaches subsection (1)(a) commits an offence and is liable on summary conviction to a fine not exceeding $10,000.

(4) A person who breaches subsection (1)(c) commits an and is liable on summary conviction to a fine not exceeding $10,000.

18 Deregistration of financial service provider

(1) The Registrar must deregister a financial service provider after a notice period in accordance with sections 19 and 20, if the Registrar is satisfied that the provider—

(a) is no longer qualified to be registered in accordance with section 13; or

(b) is not in the business of providing a financial service (at any time after the expiry of 3 months after registration); or

(c) has been registered because of a false or misleading representation or omission; or

(d) has proffered an application fee or annual confirmation fee or levy that has subsequently been dishonoured, declined, or reversed.

(2) The Registrar must deregister a financial service provider if the provider so requests in writing, with effect from any future date requested. The Registrar must notify any relevant licensing authority of this deregistration.

(3) For the purposes of this section and sections 19 and 20, notice period means 20 working days from the date of the Registrar's notification under section 19.

19 Notice of intention to deregister

(1) The Registrar must notify a financial service provider and any relevant licensing authority of the Registrar's intention to deregister the provider under section 18(1).

(2) The Registrar's notice must set out—

(a) that the Registrar intends to deregister the provider under section 18(1) (stating whichever paragraph applies); and

(b) the reasons why the Registrar considers the relevant paragraph in section 18(1) applies; and

(c) that there is a notice period before deregistration occurs during which the provider may object, under section 20, to the deregistration.

20 Objection to proposed deregistration of financial service provider

(1) During the notice period, the financial service provider may object (with reasons) to the proposed deregistration under section 18(1).

(2) If the Registrar receives an objection under subsection (1) within the notice period, the Registrar must consider the objection and must not proceed with a deregistration under section 18(1), unless the Registrar is satisfied that any of paragraphs (a) to (d) of section 18(1) applies.

21 Notification of deregistration of financial service provider

If the Registrar deregisters a financial service provider, the Registrar must notify—

(a) the financial service provider, stating the provider's right of appeal to the High Court against the deregistration under section 42; and

(b) any relevant licensing authority; and

(c) the public, by a notice that is publicly available on an Internet site (at all reasonable times) for not less than 20 working days.

22 Reregistration of financial service provider

(1) The Registrar may reregister a financial service provider who was deregistered—

(a) on the grounds set out in section 18(1)(b) if the Registrar is satisfied that the financial service provider was still in the business of providing a financial service at the time of deregistration; or

(b) on the grounds set out in section 18(1)(d) if the Registraris satisfied that the application fee or annual confirmation fee or levy has been paid.

(2) A reregistration is effective from the date of deregistration as if the deregistration had not occurred.

(3) If the Registrar reregisters a financial service provider, the Registrar must notify—

(a) the financial service provider; and

(b) any relevant licensing authority; and

(c) the public, by a notice that is publicly available on an Internet site (at all reasonable times) for not less than 20 working days.

23 Responsible financial service provider

(1) The Governor-General may, by Order in Council made on the recommendation of the Minister, declare (with or without conditions) that an entity is a responsible financial service provider.

(2) The Minister may make a recommendation under subsection (1) only if—

(a) the entity has applied to the Minister to be declared a responsible financial service provider; and

(b) the entity has affiliated entities who each would qualify to be registered as a financial service provider under section 13; and

(c) the Minister is satisfied that declaring the entity to be a responsible financial service provider is consistent with the purposes of this Act.

(3) The Order in Council must identify the affiliated entities of the responsible financial service provider.

24 Register of financial service providers

The Registrar must establish and maintain a register of financial service providers.

25 Operation of and access to register

(1) The register may be kept as an electronic register or in any other manner that the Registrar thinks fit.

(2) The register must be available for access and searching by members of the public at all times unless suspended under subsection (3).

(3) The Registrar may refuse access to the register or suspend its operation, in whole or in part,—

(a) if the Registrar considers that it is not practical to provide access to the register; or

(b) for any other reason that is prescribed by regulations made under this Act.

26 Purposes of register

The purposes of the register are—

(a) to enable the public and any person referred to in paragraph (b) to—

(i) identify registered financial service providers; and

(ii) access information about—

(A) the name and business address of a registered financial service provider; and

(B) the approved dispute resolution scheme or the reserve scheme of which a registered financial service provider is a member (if required by section 48); and

(BA) the type or types of financial service for which a financial service provider is registered; and

(C) whether a registered financial service provider provides a licensed service; and

(b) to assist any person in the exercise of the person's powers or the performance of the person's functions under this Act or any other enactment; and

(c) to conform with New Zealand's obligations under the FATF Recommendations.

27 Contents of register

The register must contain the following information about each registered person (to the extent that the information is relevant):

(a) the registered financial service provider's name and business address:

(b) the name and business address of the approved dispute resolution scheme or the reserve scheme of which the registered financial service provider is a member:

(ba) the type or types of financial service for which the registered financial service provider is registered:

(c) in relation to a licensed provider,—

(i) the relevant licensed service:

(ii) the name and business address of the relevant licensing authority:

(d) any other information prescribed in regulations.

28 Annual confirmation

(1) Each registered financial service provider must supply to the Registrar each year by the due date an annual confirmation of details relating to that provider.

(2) The annual confirmation must—

(a) be in the form (if any) required by the Registrar and be accompanied by the prescribed fee (if any) and any levy payable by the provider; and

(b) confirm that the provider is not disqualified under section 14; and

(c) contain, or be accompanied by, any other prescribed information or documents.

(3) If a registered financial service provider does not comply with subsection (1) by the due date, the Registrar may assume that the provider is no longer in the business of providing a financial service and sections 18 to 20 apply.

29 Registrar must amend register in certain circumstances

The Registrar must amend the register if—

(a) an annual confirmation contains information that is different from the information entered on the register (where the Registrar is satisfied that the situationsdescribed in section 18(1) do not apply); or

(b) a financial service provider informs the Registrar of information that is different from the information entered on the register (where the Registrar is satisfied that the situations described in section 18(1) do not apply); or

(c) a licensing authority informs the Registrar that a registered financial service provider has become a licensed provider in relation to a particular licensed service; or

(d) the Registrar is satisfied at any time that the register contains a typographical error or a mistake, or omits information supplied to the Registrar; or

(e) regulations made under this Act require the Registrar to do so in circumstances specified by the regulations.

30 Registrar may refuse to accept document

The Registrar may refuse to accept a document received by the Registrar under this Act if that document—

(a) is not in the required form (if any); or

(b) does not comply with prescribed requirements.

31 Searches of register

The register may be searched only by reference to the criteria specified in section 27(a) to (d) and any other criteria prescribed in regulations.

32 Search purposes

The register may be searched for the following purposes:

(a) by an individual, or a person with the consent of the individual, for the purpose of searching for information about that individual in accordance with the Privacy Act 1993:

(b) by a person for a purpose referred to in section 26:

(c) by a person for the purpose of advising another person in connection with any of the purposes referred to in this section.

33 When search breaches information privacy principle

A person who searches a public register for personal information for a purpose that is not a purpose set out in section 32 must be treated, for the purposes of Part 8 of the Privacy Act 1993, as if that person has breached an information privacy principle under section 66(1)(a)(i) of that Act.

34 Sharing information with other persons or bodies

(1) The Registrar may communicate to any of the persons or bodies referred to in subsection (4) any information that the Registrar—

(a) holds (other than on the register) in relation to the exercise of the Registrar's powers or the performance of the Registrar's functions and duties; and

(b) considers may assist the person or body in the exercise of its powers or the performance of its functions and duties.

(2) The Registrar may use any information communicated to the Registrar by a person or body referred to in subsection (4) in the Registrar's exercise of the Registrar's powers or the performance of the Registrar's functions and duties.

(3) This section applies despite anything to the contrary in any enactment, contract, deed, or document.

(4) The persons or bodies to which this section applies are—

(a) a licensing authority identified in Schedule 2:

(b) the New Zealand Police:

(c) the person responsible for an approved dispute resolution scheme:

(d) the person responsible for the reserve scheme:

(e) a prescribed agency that carries out supervisory or enforcement functions relating to money laundering or terrorist financing:

(f) a prescribed overseas agency that is the equivalent of the Registrar or of a body referred to in paragraphs (a) to (c), but only where there is a written agreement between the overseas agency and the Minister about sharing the information.

35 Appointment of Registrar

(1) The chief executive must appoint a Registrar of Financial Service Providers under the State Sector Act 1988.

(2) The person holding office as Registrar of Companies under the Companies Act 1993, immediately before the commencement of this Act, is deemed to have been appointed as the first Registrar of Financial Service Providers in accordance with this section.

36 Power of Registrar to delegate

(1) The Registrar may delegate to any person, either generally or particularly, any of the Registrar's functions, duties, and powers except the power of delegation.

(2) A delegation—

(a) must be in writing; and

(b) may be made subject to any restrictions and conditions the Registrar thinks fit; and

(c) is revocable at any time, in writing; and

(d) does not prevent the performance or exercise of a function, duty, or power by the Registrar.

(3) A person to whom any functions, duties, or powers are delegated may perform and exercise them in the same manner and with the same effect as if they had been conferred directly by this Act and not by delegation.

(4) A person who appears to act under a delegation is presumed to be acting in accordance with its terms in the absence of evidence to the contrary.

37 Registrar's inspection powers

(1) The Registrar, or a person authorised by the Registrar, may take any of the steps listed in subsection (2) for the purpose of ascertaining whether a person—

(a) is in the business of providing a financial service in breach of section 11; or

(b) is holding out or has held out that the person is in the business of providing a financial service in breach of section 12; or

(c) is qualified or has been qualified to be registered in accordance with section 13; or

(d) has made a false or misleading representation or omission in breach of section 41.

(2) The steps referred to in subsection (1) are the following:

(a) requiring a person to produce for inspection relevant documents within that person's possession or control:

(b) inspecting and taking copies of relevant documents:

(c) taking possession of relevant documents and retaining them for a reasonable time for the purpose of taking copies.

(3) Any person who exercises powers under subsection (1) must make his or her authorisation from the Registrar available on request.

(4) Nothing in this section limits or affects the Tax Administration Act 1994 or the Statistics Act 1975.

(5) A person must not obstruct or hinder the exercise of a power conferred by subsection (1).

(6) If a registered financial service provider does not comply with a requirement under subsection (2)(a) within 20 working days from the date the requirement was notified to the provider, the Registrar may assume that the provider

is no longer in the business of providing a financial service and sections 18 to 20 apply.

(7) A person who knowingly fails to comply with a requirement under subsection (2) commits an offence and is liable on summary conviction,—

(a) in the case of an individual, to a fine not exceeding $30,000:

(b) in the case of a person who is not an individual, to a fine not exceeding $300,000.

(8) A person who breaches subsection (5) commits an offence and is liable on summary conviction,—

(a) in the case of an individual, to a fine not exceeding $30,000:

(b) in the case of a person who is not an individual, to a fine not exceeding $300,000.

(9) In this section, relevant document means a document that contains information relating to whether a person—

(a) is in the business of providing a financial service or a particular financial service; or

(b) is holding out or has held out that the person is in the business of providing a financial service in breach of section 12; or

(c) is qualified or has been qualified to be registered in accordance with section 13; or

(d) has made a false or misleading representation or omission in breach of section 41.

38 Disclosure of information and reports

(1) A person authorised by the Registrar for the purposes of section 37 who has obtained a document or information in the course of making an inspection under that section or prepared a report in relation to an inspection under that section must, if directed to do so by the Registrar, give the document, information, or report to—

(a) the Registrar; or

(b) the Minister; or

(c) the chief executive; or

(d) any person authorised by the Registrar to receive the document, information, or report for the purposes of this Act.

(2) A person authorised by the Registrar for the purposes of section 37 who has obtained a document or information in the course of making an inspection under that section or prepared a report in relation to an inspection under that section must not disclose that document, information, or report, except—

(a) in accordance with subsection (1); or

(b) subject to the approval of the Registrar, with the consent of the person to whom it relates; or

(c) subject to the approval of the Registrar, for the purposes of this Act; or

(d) to the extent that the information, or information contained in the document or report, is available under any Act or in a public document.

(3) A person who fails to comply with this section commits an offence and is liable on summary conviction to a fine not exceeding $10,000.

39 Exercise of powers under section 37 not affected by appeal

(1) Despite any other provision of any Act or any rule of law, if a person appeals or applies to the High Court in relation to an act or decision of the Registrar or a person authorised by the Registrar under section 37, until a decision on the appeal or application is given,—

(a) the Registrar, or that authorised person, may continue to exercise the powers under that section as if no such appeal or application had been made; and

(b) no person is excused from fulfilling an obligation under that section by reason of that appeal or application.

(2) Subsection (3) overrides subsection (1).

(3) If the appeal or application is allowed or granted,—

(a) the Registrar must ensure that, as soon as is reasonably practicable after the court's decision is delivered, any copy of a document taken or retained under section 37 is destroyed; and

(b) no information acquired under section 37 is admissible in evidence in any proceedings unless the court hearing the proceedings in which it is sought to adduce the evidence is satisfied it was not obtained unfairly.

40 Offence also committed by director

If any financial service provider that is not an individual commits an offence against this Act, every director of the provider who knowingly authorises or knowingly fails to prevent the offence also commits an offence against this Act.

41 Offence to make false or misleading representation

(1) Every person commits an offence who, in any document or information required by or for the purposes of this Part or by regulations (whether or not supplied to the Registrar),—

(a) makes a representation knowing that it is false or misleading in a material particular; or

(b) omits any matter knowing that the omission is false or misleading in a material particular.

(2) A person who is convicted of an offence under subsection (1) is liable on summary conviction,—

(a) in the case of an individual, to imprisonment for a term not exceeding 2 years or to a fine not exceeding $100,000, or to both; or

(b) in the case of a person who is not an individual, to a fine not exceeding $300,000.

42 Appeals from Registrar's decisions

(1) A financial service provider who is not satisfied with any of the following decisions of the Registrar may appeal to the High Court:

(a) not registering an applicant as a financial service provider under section 16:

(b) a deregistration under section 18:

(c) a decision of the Registrar or a person authorised by the Registrar under section 37.

(2) The time within which an appeal under subsection (1) may be made is 20 working days after the date of notification of the decision, or within any further time that the court allows.

(3) On appeal, the court may do any of the following:

(a) confirm, modify, or reverse the decision or any part of it:

(b) exercise any of the powers that could have been exercised by the Registrar in relation to the matter to which the appeal relates:

(c) refer the decision back to the Registrar with directions to reconsider the whole or a specified part of the act or decision.

43 Decisions continue in effect until appeal

Unless the High Court orders otherwise, a decision appealed against under section 42 continues in effect.

44 Regulations under Part 1 and this Part

(1) The Governor-General may, by Order in Council on the recommendation of the Minister, make regulations for all or any of the following purposes:

(aa) declaring a class of contract to be a contract of insurance for the purposes of this Act:

(a) prescribing a financial service for the purposes of section 5(n):

(ab) exempting any service or person or class of service or persons from the application of this Act, and prescribing the terms and conditions (if any) of the exemption:

(b) specifying information or documents to be included in, or provided with, applications, and requiring documents to be signed by specified persons:

(c) prescribing procedures, requirements, and other matters, not inconsistent with this Part or with the purposes described in section 26, relating to the register, including matters that relate to—

(i) the operation of the register:

(ii) the information or documents to be contained in the register:

(iii) access to the register:

(iv) search criteria for the register:

(v) fees that may be payable in order to search the register:

(d) prescribing either of the following types of agency:

(i) an agency that carries out supervisory or enforcement functions relating to money laundering or terrorist financing for the purposes of section 34; or (ii an overseas agency that is the equivalent of the Registrar or of a body referred to in section 34(4)(a) to (c) for the purposes of section 34:

(e) prescribing fees payable to the Registrar in respect of any matter under this Act or the manner in which fees may be calculated:

(f) providing for any other matters contemplated by Part 1 or by this Part, necessary for its administration, or necessary for giving it full effect.

(1A) The Minister must, in relation to a recommendation under subsection (1)(ab),—

(a) before making a recommendation, have regard to New Zealand's obligations under the FATF Recommendations; and

(b) not make the recommendation unless the Minister is satisfied that the costs of compliance with this Act would be unreasonable or not justified by the benefit of compliance.

(2) Without limiting subsection (1)(b), information or documents may be prescribed under that subsection for the purpose of assisting any person with the person's powers, functions, or duties as a licensing authority under the relevant enactment identified in Schedule 2 (regardless of whether or not that information or documentation is collected for the purposes of this Part).

(3) The Registrar may refuse to perform a function or exercise a power until a prescribed fee or levy is paid.

(4) Any Order in Council made under subsection (1)(e) may—

(a) prescribe the method of payment of a fee; and

(b) authorise the Registrar to refund or waive, in whole or in part and on any prescribed conditions, payment of a fee in relation to any person or class of persons.

(5) Any fee or amount payable to the Registrar is recoverable by the Registrar in any court of competent jurisdiction as a debt due to the Registrar.

45 Ministry must review and report on operation of this Part

(1) The Ministry must, not later than 5 years after the commencement of this section,—

(a) review the operation of this Part since the commencement of this section; and

(b) prepare a report on the review for the Minister.

(2) The report on the review must include recommendations to the Minister on whether any amendments to the Act concerning the matters dealt with in this Part are necessary or desirable.

(3) As soon as practicable after receiving the report, the Minister must present a copy of that report to the House of Representatives.

46 Territorial scope

[Repealed]

Part 3
Dispute Resolution

47 Purpose of this Part

The purpose of this Part is to promote confidence in financial service providers by improving consumers' access to redress from providers through schemes to resolve disputes. The schemes are intended to be accessible, independent, fair, accountable, efficient, and effective.

48 Financial service provider must be member of dispute resolution scheme

(1) Every financial service provider must be a member of either an approved dispute resolution scheme, or the reserve scheme, in respect of a financial service provided to a retail client.

(2) A member, in relation to an approved dispute resolution scheme or the reserve scheme, is a financial service provider who may be the subject of a complaint to that scheme.

(3) However, this obligation does not apply—

(a) to a financial service provider if—

(i) it is in the business of providing financial services only because it is an issuer or promoter participating in 1 or more offers of securities to the public; and

(ii) doing so is not its only or principal business; or

(b) to a financial service provider if it is exempted from the obligation by or under any other Act or by regulations made under section 79.

49 Who are retail clients

(1) A retail client is any person who receives a financial service who is not a wholesale client.

(2) The following persons who receive a financial service are wholesale clients in respect of that financial service:

(a) a person who is in the business of providing any financial service and receives the financial service in the course of that business:

(b) a person whose principal business is the investment of money or who, in the course of and for the purposes of the person's business, habitually invests money:

(c) an entity to which at least 1 of the following applied at the end of each of the last 2 completed accounting periods:

(i) at the balance date, the net assets of the entity exceeded $1 million:

(ii) the turnover of the entity for the accounting period exceeded $1 million:

(d) a related body corporate (within the meaning of section 5B(2) of the Securities Markets Act 1988) of an entity to which paragraph (c) applies:

(e) a local authority, a Crown entity, a State enterprise, the Reserve Bank of New Zealand, and the National Provident Fund (and a company appointed under clause 3(1)(b) of Schedule 4 of the National Provident Fund Restructuring Act 1990):

(f) a person who falls within 1 or more of the categories listed in section 3(2), 5(2CB), or 5(2CBA) of the Securities Act 1978 if the service relates to securities that may be offered to that person, or that have been subscribed for by that person, in a private offer of securities:

(g) an eligible investor under section 49A:

(h) if the financial service is a financial adviser service or a broking service, a person who is a wholesale client in respect of that service under the Financial Advisers Act 2008.

(3) If subsection (2) applies to a person (A), it applies equally to any controlling owner, director, employee, agent, or other person acting in the course of, and for the purposes of, A's business to the same extent as it applies to A.

(4) In this section,—

entity—

(a) includes a body corporate and an unincorporated body (including partners in a partnership, members of a joint venture, or the trustees of a trust) and the sole trustee of a trust acting in his, her, or its capacity as trustee of that trust; but

(b) does not include an individual

private offer of securities means an offer of securities that—

(a) does not constitute an offer of securities to the public under section 3 of the Securities Act 1978; or

(b) is exempt from Part 2 (other than sections 38B and 58) of that Act under section 5(2CB) or 5(2CBA) of that Act.

49A Who are eligible investors

(1) A client is an eligible investor if—

(a) the client certifies in writing that the client understands that, as a consequence of certifying himself, herself, or itself to be an eligible investor, the financial service provider may not be a member of an approved dispute resolution scheme; and

(b) the client states the reasons for this certification; and

(c) a financial service provider signs a written acceptance of the certification in accordance with section 49B.

(2) A certification may be specific to a particular service or class of services or may be general (but is effective only in relation to services provided after all of the requirements of subsection (1)(a) to (c) are met).

49B Acceptance of certification

(1) A financial service provider must not accept a certification unless he, she, or it, having considered the client's reasons for the certification,—

(a) is satisfied that the client has been sufficiently advised of the consequences of the certification; and

(b) has no reason to believe that the certification is incorrect or that further information or investigation is required as to whether or not the certification is correct.

(2) The person who accepts the certification of a client may be the person providing the financial services to the client (but does not need to be).

(3) A financial service provider who accepts a certification without having complied with subsection (1) contravenes a wholesale certification requirement.

(4) Contravention of this section may give rise to a pecuniary penalty order or compensatory order (see sections 79A and 79B).

49C Revocation of certification

(1) A client who is an eligible investor may revoke a certification, in relation to a financial service provider to whom the certification has been given, by giving the financial service provider a signed notification to that effect.

(2) A revocation is effective only in relation to services provided after it is given.

49D How to opt out of being wholesale client

(1) A person may opt out of being a wholesale client, in relation to a financial service provider, by giving the financial service provider a signed notification to that effect.

(2) A notification may be specific to a particular service, or class of services, or may be general for all services provided by the financial service provider to whom it is given.

(3) A person may vary or revoke a notification in the same way as the notification may be given.

(4) A notification (or variation or revocation of a notification) under this section is effective only in relation to services provided after it is given.

(5) This section does not apply if a person is a wholesale client by reason of being an eligible investor.

49E Giving revocation of certification or notification of opt out

(1) A revocation of a certification under section 49C or a notification under section 49D is sufficiently given to a financial service provider if—

(a) it is provided to the financial service provider; or

(b) delivered or posted to the financial service provider at the person's business address stated on the register or (if not registered) the person's last known place of business in New Zealand; or

(c) sent by fax or email to the person's fax number or email address stated on the register.

(2) The revocation or notification is treated as received by the person no later than 7 days after it is posted or 2 days after it is faxed or emailed, unless the person to whom it is posted or sent proves that it was not received (otherwise than through fault on the person's part).

49F Members of dispute resolution scheme must comply with rules and binding resolutions

(1) A member of an approved dispute resolution scheme or the reserve scheme must comply with the rules of the scheme.

(2) On the application of the person responsible for the scheme, a District Court may make an order requiring a member of the scheme to do either or both of the following:

(a) comply with the rules of the scheme:

(b) comply with a resolution of a complaint that constitutes a binding resolution under those rules (a binding settlement).

(3) If a District Court is satisfied that the terms of a binding settlement of a complaint are manifestly unreasonable, the court's order under subsection (2) may modify the terms of the binding settlement.

(4) If an order requiring a member to comply with a binding settlement includes a requirement that the member pay an amount of money to a person, that order (or part of the order) may be enforced as if it were a judgment by a District Court for the payment of a sum of money.

49G Offence to fail to comply with District Court order

(1) A member of an approved dispute resolution scheme or the reserve scheme who, knowing that the member is subject to an order made under section 49F, fails to comply with the order, or fails to comply with the order within the time or in the manner required by the order, commits an offence and is liable on summary conviction to a fine not exceeding $200,000.

(2) Nothing in this section applies to an order or part of an order of a District Court referred to in section 49F(4).

50 Meaning of approved dispute resolution scheme

A dispute resolution scheme is an approved dispute resolution scheme if it has been approved by the Minister in accordance with this Part and that approval has not been withdrawn.

51 Application for approval

(1) The person responsible for a dispute resolution scheme may apply to the Minister for approval of the scheme.

(2) The applicant must submit the following with the application:

(a) the rules about the scheme:

(b) any other information that is prescribed concerning the considerations outlined in section 52:

(c) the prescribed fee (if any).

(3) The Minister may request the applicant to supply further information or documentation relating to the matters referred to in subsection (2)(a) or (b).

52 Mandatory considerations for approval

(1) When considering an application under section 51, the Minister must have regard to the following considerations in light of the principles listed in subsection (2):

(a) whether the scheme has an appropriate purpose:

(b) whether the applicant has undertaken reasonable consultation on the scheme with members or potential members of the scheme, and persons (or their representatives) likely to be substantially affected by the scheme:

(c) whether the applicant has adequate funding to enable it to operate the scheme according to the scheme's purpose and in accordance with the rules about the scheme:

(d) whether the applicant's directors and senior managers are competent to manage a dispute resolution scheme:

(e) whether the scheme is capable of resolving disputes about the types of financial services provided by the members or potential members of the scheme:

(f) the amounts of money that complaints lodged with the scheme may be about, and whether those amounts are reasonable and appropriate:

(g) whether the rules about the scheme are adequate and comply with—

(i) the principles listed in subsection (2); and

(ii) the requirements of section 63:

(h) the number of currently approved dispute resolution schemes:

(i) the types of financial service providers that may be members of currently approved dispute resolution schemes:

(j) the proposed size of the scheme:

(k) the types of financial service providers that may be potential members of the scheme:

(l) any other applications for approval that have been made.

(2) The principles are—

(a) accessibility:

(b) independence:

(c) fairness:

(d) accountability:

(e) efficiency:

(f) effectiveness.

53 Minister must decide application for approval

(1) The Minister must decide an application under section 51 by approving it or by rejecting it.

(2) The Minister may only make a decision under subsection (1) after consultation with—

(a) the Minister of Finance; and

(b) the Minister of Commerce.

54 Notification and publication of decision

The Minister must, as soon as practicable after deciding the application,—

(a) notify the applicant of the decision; and

(b) if the decision is to approve the application, ensure that—

(i) the approval is published in the Gazette; and

(ii) the chief executive updates the details described in section 78(2).

55 Reapplication by unsuccessful applicant

An applicant whose application has been rejected may at any time reapply under section 51.

56 Withdrawal of approval

(1) The Minister may withdraw the approval of an approved dispute resolution scheme after a notice period in accordance with sections 57 and 58 for any or all of the following reasons:

(a) there has been a breach of a prescribed requirement:

(b) there has been a failure to comply with the rules about the scheme:

(c) the person responsible for the scheme has not maintained or published a list of current members as required by section 62:

(d) the person responsible for the scheme has not published the rules as required by section 64:

(e) the person responsible for the scheme has not supplied the Minister with any of the following:

(i) an annual report as required by section 68:

(ii) any further information requested by the Minister under section 69:

(iii) an independent review as required by the rule described in section 63(q):

(f) the person responsible for the scheme has not notified the Minister in accordance with section 65 before changing the rules about the scheme:

(g) the person responsible for the scheme has not complied with section 67:

(h) the scheme no longer satisfies the principles in section 52(2).

(2) When considering whether to withdraw an approval, the Minister must have regard to the considerations referred to in section 52(1)(a) to (g) in light of the principles listed in section 52(2).

(3) The Minister must withdraw the approval of an approved dispute resolution scheme if the person responsible for the scheme so requests, with effect from any future date requested.

(4) For the purposes of this section and sections 57 and 58, notice period means 20 working days from the date of the Minister's notification under section 57(1).

57 Notice of intention to withdraw approval

(1) The Minister must notify the person responsible for the approved dispute resolution scheme of the Minister's intention to withdraw the scheme's approval under section 56(1).

(2) The Minister's notice must set out—

(a) that the Minister intends to withdraw the scheme's approval for any or all of the grounds described in section 56(1) (stating which apply); and

(b) the reasons why the Minister considers any or all of the grounds described in section 56(1) apply; and

(c) that there is a notice period before the withdrawal of the scheme's approval during which the person responsible for the scheme may object, under section 58, to the intended withdrawal.

(3) The Minister's notice may require the person responsible for the scheme to—

(a) notify all members of the Minister's intention to withdraw the scheme's approval; or

(b) provide the Minister with a list of the names and business addresses of current members so that the Minister can, if the Minister wishes, notify all members of the Minister's intention to withdraw the scheme's approval.

58 Objection to intended withdrawal of approval

(1) During the notice period, the person responsible for an approved dispute resolution scheme—

(a) may object (with reasons) to the intended withdrawal of the scheme's approval under section 56(1); and

(b) must not accept any new members.

(2) If the Minister has received an objection under subsection (1) within the notice period, the Minister must consider it and must not proceed with a withdrawal under section 56(1) unless the Minister is satisfied that any or all of the reasons set out in 56(1) apply.

59 Approval is withdrawn from date person responsible for scheme is notified

If the Minister withdraws a scheme's approval, the scheme's approval is withdrawn from the date the person responsible for the scheme is notified under section 60(a).

60 Notification and publication of withdrawal of approval

The Minister must, as soon as practicable after withdrawing the approval of a dispute resolution scheme,—

(a) notify the person responsible for the scheme; and

(b) notify the Registrar; and

(c) ensure the withdrawal is published in the Gazette; and

(d) ensure the chief executive updates the details described in section 78(2).

61 Effect of withdrawal of approval on members of dispute resolution scheme

On the date that a dispute resolution scheme's approval is withdrawn, members of the scheme become members of the reserve scheme.

62 List of members

The person responsible for an approved dispute resolution scheme must maintain a list of the scheme's current members and must publish this list on an Internet site that is publicly available (at all reasonable times).

63 Rules about approved dispute resolution scheme

The person responsible for an approved dispute resolution scheme must issue rules about that scheme, and those rules must provide for, or set out, the following:

(a) which types of financial service providers may be members of the scheme (all providers of that type must be eligible):

(b) how financial service providers become members of the scheme and how membership is terminated:

(c) that consumers and businesses that have no more than 19 full-time equivalent employees may make complaints for resolution by the scheme:

(d) how complaints about a member may be made for resolution by the scheme:

(e) a period after which the scheme, if asked by a complainant, must investigate a complaint that has been made directly to a member:

(f) that complaints about members must be investigated in a way that is consistent with the rules of natural justice:

(g) that the scheme has jurisdiction in respect of a breach of contract, statutory obligation, or industry code, or any other matter provided for in the rules:

(h) that any information may be considered in relation to a complaint and any inquiry made that is fair and reasonable in the circumstances:

(i) the remedial action that the scheme can impose on a member to resolve a complaint (for example, a requirement to change systems or to compensate a complainant up to a certain amount stated in the rules):

(j) how remedial action may be enforced against the scheme's members, including after members have left the scheme:

(k) that a financial service provider who has not taken remedial action imposed on that provider by another approved dispute resolution scheme or the reserve scheme cannot join the scheme:

(l) that the scheme will not charge a fee to any complainant to investigate or resolve a complaint:

(m) that a resolution of a complaint about a member of the scheme is binding on the member concerned:

(n) that a resolution of a complaint about a member of the scheme is binding on the complainant concerned, if the complainant accepts the resolution:

(o) that the complainant may take alternative court action against the member at any time, including if the complainant rejects the resolution:

(p) that the scheme may cease investigating and resolving a complaint if the complainant takes alternative court action against the member:

(q) that an independent review of the scheme must occur at least once every 5 years after the date of the scheme's approval and must be supplied to the Minister within 3 months of completion:

(r) that the person responsible for the scheme and the scheme's members must inform the people referred to in paragraph (c) about the scheme.

64 Obligation to publish rules

The person responsible for an approved dispute resolution scheme must make copies of the rules about the scheme available for inspection by the public, free of charge,—

(a) at the scheme's head office (during ordinary office hours); and

(b) on an Internet site in an electronic form that is publicly available (at all reasonable times).

65 Duty to notify change to rules

The person responsible for an approved dispute resolution scheme must notify the Minister if the person wishes to change the rules about the scheme.

66 Minister's consideration of change of rules

(1) After receiving a notification under section 65, the Minister may notify the person responsible for a scheme that the Minister—

(a) approves the change; or

(b) considers the proposed change is not adequate and does not comply with—

(i) the principles listed in section 52(2); and

(ii) the requirements of section 63.

(2) If subsection (1)(b) applies, the rule change must not be made.

(3) If the Minister does not notify the person responsible for the scheme in accordance with subsection (1) within 45 working days of the notification of the change of rules, the change is treated as having been approved by the Minister.

67 Duty to co-operate and communicate information in certain circumstances

The person responsible for an approved dispute resolution scheme must—

(a) co-operate with other approved dispute resolution schemes and with the reserve scheme if a complaint involves members of those other schemes (disclosing personal information in accordance with the Privacy Act 1993 and protecting information that is subject to an obligation of confidence); and

(b) co-operate with the Registrar, including by communicating information to the Registrar in accordance with sections 17 and 34; and

(c) if there is a series of material complaints about a particular licensed provider or class of licensed provider, communicate that fact to the relevant licensing authority:

(d) if there is a series of material complaints about a particular broker or class of broker, communicate that fact to the Financial Markets Authority.

68 Annual report

The person responsible for an approved dispute resolution scheme must supply to the Minister, within 3 months after the end of the financial year applying to the scheme, an annual report containing prescribed information about the scheme in relation to that financial year.

69 Person responsible for approved dispute resolution scheme must supply further information on Minister's request

(1) The person responsible for an approved dispute resolution scheme must supply to the Minister—

(a) any further information requested by the Minister about the information that is required by regulations to be in an annual report; and

(b) any information requested by the Minister about the scheme's compliance with the principles listed in section 52(2).

(2) In supplying the information to the Minister, the person must disclose personal information in accordance with the Privacy Act 1993 and protect information that is subject to an obligation of confidentiality.

70 Annual report and information requested by Minister to be publicly available

The person responsible for an approved dispute resolution scheme must make copies of its annual report available for inspection by the public, free of charge,—

(a) at the scheme's head office (during ordinary office hours); and

(b) on an Internet site in an electronic form that is publicly available (at all reasonable times).

71 Reserve scheme

reserve scheme is a dispute resolution scheme that has been appointed by Order in Council under section 72 to fulfill the functions of the reserve scheme.

72 Appointment of reserve scheme

(1) The Governor-General may, by Order in Council made on the recommendation of the Minister,—

(a) appoint a dispute resolution scheme to fulfil the functions of the reserve scheme (with or without conditions) for a term recommended by the Minister; and

(b) prescribe rules about the functions of the reserve scheme; and

(c) prescribe rules about the funding of the reserve scheme (see section 72A).

(2) Rules made under subsection (1)(b) must provide for equivalent matters to those required by section 63 to be provided for, or set out, in the rules of an approved dispute resolution scheme.

(3) The Minister may make a recommendation only if—

(a) the person responsible for the scheme consents in writing to the scheme being appointed to fulfil the functions of the reserve scheme in accordance with the rules made under subsection (1)(b); and

(b) the Minister is satisfied that the person responsible for the scheme and the scheme itself are capable of resolving disputes relating to all types of providers of all types of financial services; and

(c) the Minister is satisfied that the scheme is a formally constituted dispute resolution body with demonstrable experience; and

(d) the Minister is satisfied that the person responsible for the scheme and the scheme itself are capable of fulfilling the functions of the reserve scheme in accordance with the rules made under subsection (1)(b).

(4) The Minister may recommend an Order in Council described in subsection (1)(a) only after consultation with—

(a) the Minister of Finance; and

(b) the Minister of Commerce.

(5) The Minister may recommend an Order in Council described in subsection (1)(b) only after consultation with—

(a) the Minister of Finance; and

(b) the Minister of Commerce; and

(c) any persons (or their representatives) that the Minister considers are likely to be substantially affected by the recommendation.

(6) A failure to comply with subsection (5)(c) does not affect the validity of an Order in Council made under subsection (1).

(7) Conditions that may be imposed by an Order in Council may relate to any or all of the following:

(a) the governance arrangements relating to the reserve scheme:

(b) other prescribed matters that relate to the principles listed in section 52(2).

(8) The Minister's first recommendation for an Order in Council referred to in subsection (1) must be made within 2 years of this section coming into force.

72A Reserve scheme: rules about fees and charges

(1) Rules made under section 72(1)(c) may—

(a) provide for an applicant for membership, or for renewal of membership, to pay a fee in respect of the application:

(b) require members to pay a membership fee:

(c) if a complaint is made about a member, require the member to pay a charge in respect of the complaint in circumstances provided in the rules:

(d) exempt a person or class of persons from liability to pay a fee or charge in whole or in part:

(e) provide for the refund or waiver of a fee or charge, in whole or in part, for a person or class of persons:

(f) provide for the termination of the membership of a member who fails to pay a fee or charge within the period provided in the rules.

(2) The charge under subsection (1)(c) may be—

(a) a fixed amount; or

(b) an amount calculated by reference to the costs of investigating and determining the complaint; or

(c) a combination of the amounts referred to in paragraphs (a) and (b).

(3) Rules for the purposes of this section may make different provision for different classes of financial service provider.

73 Revocation of appointment as reserve scheme

(1) The Governor-General may, by Order in Council made on the recommendation of the Minister, revoke an appointment made under section 72(1)(a).

(2) The Minister may make a recommendation only for any or all of the following reasons:

(a) has been a failure to fulfil the functions of the reserve scheme as required by rules made under section 72(1)(b):

(b) there has been a breach of a condition of appointment:

(c) the person responsible for the reserve scheme requests that the scheme's appointment as the reserve scheme be revoked.

(3) The Minister may make a recommendation for the reasons set out in subsection (2)(a) or (b) only after consultation with—

(a) the Minister of Finance; and

(b) the Minister of Commerce.

(4) At the same time as making a recommendation under subsection (1), the Minister must recommend that the Governor-General appoint another dispute resolution scheme to fulfil the functions of the reserve scheme under section 72(1)(a) for a term recommended by the Minister.

74 Notice of intention to recommend revocation of appointment as reserve scheme under section 73(2)(a) or (b)

(1) The Minister must notify the person responsible for the reserve scheme that the Minister intends, under section 73(2)(a) or (b), to recommend a revocation of the reserve scheme's appointment.

2) The Minister's notice must set out—

(a) that the Minister intends, under section 73(2)(a) or (b), to recommend a revocation of the reserve scheme's appointment; and

(b) the reasons why the Minister considers that section 73(2)(a) or (b) apply; and

(c) that there is a notice period during which the person responsible for the reserve scheme may object, under section 75, to the intended recommendation.

(3) For the purposes of this section and section 75, notice period means 20 working days from the date of the Minister's notification under subsection (1).

75 Objection to intended recommendation for revocation

(1) During the notice period, the person responsible for the reserve scheme may object (with reasons) to the Minster's intention, under section 73(2)(a) or (b), to recommend a revocation of the reserve scheme's appointment.

(2) If the Minister has received an objection under subsection (1) within the notice period, the Minister must consider the objection and must not proceed with a recommendation for a revocation of the reserve scheme's appointment under section 73(2)(a) or (b) unless the Minister is satisfied that section 73(2)(a) or (b) apply.

76 Duty to co-operate and communicate information in certain circumstances

The person responsible for a reserve scheme must—

(a) co-operate with approved dispute resolution schemes if a complaint involves members of those schemes (disclosing personal information in accordance with the Privacy Act 1993 and protecting information that is subject to an obligation of confidence); and

(b) co-operate with the Registrar, including by communicating information to the Registrar in accordance with sections 17 and 34; and

(c) if there is a series of material complaints about a particular licensed provider or class of licensed provider, communicate that fact to the relevant licensing authority:

(d) if there is a series of material complaints about a particular broker or class of broker, communicate that fact to the Financial Markets Authority.

77 Levy to fund reserve scheme

[Repealed]

78 Publication of details relating to approved dispute resolution schemes and reserve scheme

(1) The chief executive—

(a) must ensure that the details described in subsection (2) are available for inspection by the public, free of charge, at the head office of the Ministry (during ordinary office hours), and on an Internet site that is publicly available (at all reasonable times):

(b) may make copies of the details available in any other way that the chief executive considers appropriate in the circumstances.

(2) The details are—

(a) the names of approved dispute resolution schemes and the name and business address of the person responsible for each scheme; and

(b) the name of the reserve scheme and the name and business address of the person responsible for the reserve scheme.

78A Levy

(1) The Governor-General may, by Order in Council made on the recommendation of the Minister, make regulations requiring registered financial service providers (or a prescribed class of financial service providers) to pay a levy to the Minister.

(2) The purpose of the levy is to meet, in whole or in part, the costs of—

(a) the Ministry's functions under this Part (including the costs of collecting the levy); and

(b) the reserve scheme (to the extent that these are not met by fees and charges imposed in rules made under section 72(1)(c)).

(3) Regulations under this section may—

(a) specify an amount payable as the levy or amethod of calculating or ascertaining the levy (which may be based on the estimated costs):

(b) include or provide for including in the levy any shortfall in recovering the actual costs:

(c) refund or provide for refunds of any over-recovery of those actual costs:

(d) specify the financial year or part financial year to which the levy applies, and apply the levy to that financial year and each subsequent financial year until the levy is revoked or repealed:

(e) for the first financial year to which the levy applies, include in the levy costs from 1 January 2009:

(f) require payment of a levy for a financial year or part financial year irrespective of the fact that the regulations may be made after that financial year has commenced:

(g) provide for the collection and payment of the levy, including the time by which the levy must be paid:

(h) exempt a person or class of persons from liability to pay the levy, in whole or in part:

(i) provide for a waiver or refund of the levy, in whole or in part, for a person or class of persons:

(j) provide for interest to be paid if a person fails to pay the levy by the due date.

(4) Regulations under this section may make different provision for different classes of registered financial service providers including, without limitation, for—

(a) members of the reserve scheme:

(b) members of approved dispute resolution schemes:

(c) those who provide different types of financial service.

(5) The levy is recoverable as a debt due to the Crown.

(6) Before making a recommendation under subsection (1), the Minister must consult with persons or representatives of persons that the Minister considers are likely to be substantially affected by the proposed regulations.

7) A failure to comply with subsection (6) does not affect the validity of the regulations.

79 Regulations under this Part

(1) The Governor-General may, by Order in Council made on the recommendation of the Minister, make regulations for all or any of the following purposes:

(a) exempting any person or class of persons from the obligation to be a member of either an approved dispute resolution scheme or the reserve scheme, and prescribing the terms and conditions (if any) of the exemption:

(b) prescribing the information or documents to be supplied to the Minister as part of an application under this Part:

(c) prescribing processes for applications for the approval of dispute resolution schemes:

(d) prescribing rules for a class of approved dispute resolution scheme or for all approved dispute resolution schemes in the event that approval of those schemes is withdrawn:

(e) prescribing the information that must be included in every annual report supplied in accordance with section 68, which must include—

  (i) information about any independent review that occurred within the previous 12 months; and

  (ii) information about a scheme's operation (including complaints received):

f) prescribing fees payable in respect of any matter under this Part or the manner in which fees may be calculated:

(g) providing for any other matters contemplated by this Part, necessary for its administration, or necessary for giving it full effect.

(1A) The Minister must not recommend the making of regulations under subsection (1)(a), unless the Minister is satisfied that—

(a) the exemption is consistent with the purposes of this Act; and

(b) the costs of compliance with the obligation would be unreasonable or not justified by the benefits of compliance.

(2) The Minister may refuse to make a decision under this Part until the prescribed fee is paid.

(3) Any Order in Council made under subsection (1) may—

(a) prescribe the method of payment of a fee; and

(b) authorise the Minister to refund or waive, in whole or in part and on any prescribed conditions, payment of a fee in relation to any person or class of persons.

(4) Any fee or amount payable under this Part is recoverable in any court of competent jurisdiction as a debt due to the Crown.

79A Pecuniary order for contravening wholesale certification requirement

(1) The High Court may, on application by the Financial Markets Authority, order a person to pay a pecuniary penalty to the Crown if the court is satisfied that the person has, without reasonable excuse, contravened a wholesale certification requirement under section 49B.

(2) The amount of the pecuniary penalty must not, in respect of each act or omission, exceed $100,000 in the case of an individual or $300,000 in the case of an entity.

(3) In setting the amount of the pecuniary penalty, the court must take into account all of the following matters:

(a) the nature and extent of the contravention:

(b) the nature and extent of any loss or damage suffered by a person as a result of the contravention, including the effect on a person of the loss of the opportunity to make a complaint to an approved dispute resolution scheme or the reserve scheme:

(c) the circumstances in which the contravention took place (including whether the contravention was intentional, inadvertent, or caused by negligence):

(d) whether the person has previously been found by the court in proceedings under this Act to have engaged in similar conduct.

(4) A financial service provider may not be liable to more than 1 pecuniary penalty in respect of the same conduct.

(5) Proceedings under this section may be commenced at any time within 3 years after the contravention occurred.

79B Compensation for contravention of wholesale certification requirement

(1) If the court orders a person to pay a pecuniary penalty under section 79A in respect of the contravention of a wholesale certification requirement, the court may, in addition, order a person to pay compensation to any person who has

suffered, or is likely to suffer, loss or damage as a result of the contravention (the aggrieved person).

(2) An application for orders under this section may be made by the Financial Markets Authority or any aggrieved person.

(3) The application must be made within 1 year of the date of the pecuniary penalty order.

(4) The court may make an order under this section whether or not any aggrieved person is a party to the proceedings.

(5) In proceedings under this section, the court may make such orders as it thinks fit.

80 Ministry must review and report on operation of this Part

(1) The Ministry must, not later than 5 years after the commencement of this section,—

(a) review the operation of this Part since the commencement of this section; and

(b) prepare a report on the review for the Minister.

(2) The report on the review must include recommendations to the Minister on whether any amendments to the Act concerning the matters dealt with in this Part are necessary or desirable.

(3) As soon as practicable after receiving the report, the Minister must present a copy of that report to the House of Representatives.

81 Consequential amendment

The enactment specified in Schedule 1 is amended in the manner indicated in that schedule.

Schedule 1
Consequential amendment

Privacy Act 1993 (1993 No 28)

Part 1 of Schedule 2: insert the following item in its appropriate alphabetical order:

Financial Service Providers (Registration and Dispute Resolution) Act 2008 Section 24

Schedule 2
Licensing authorities and licensed providers

This schedule identifies—

(a) bodies who are licensing authorities; and

(b) the persons that each licensing authority licenses, registers, authorises, or otherwise approves to provide a licensed service; and

(c) the enactments that require the relevant financial service to be provided only by a person who is licensed, registered, authorised, or otherwise approved by that licensing authority.

Licensing authority	Licensed provider	Enactment
Financial Markets Authority	Authorised financial advisers and qualifying financial entities	Financial Advisers Act 2008
Reserve Bank of New Zealand	Registered banks	Reserve Bank of New Zealand Act 1989
Financial Markets Authority	Licensed trustees in respect of debt securities, licensed statutory supervisors in respect of participatory securities, and licensed unit trustees	Securities Trustees and Statutory Supervisors Act 2011

Financial Service Providers (Registration) Regulations 2010

(SR 2010/235)

Anand Satyanand, Governor-General

Order in Council

At Wellington this 9th day of August 2010

Present:

His Excellency the Governor-General in Council

Pursuant to section 44 of the Financial Service Providers (Registration and Dispute Resolution) Act 2008, His Excellency the Governor-General, acting on the advice and with the consent of the Executive Council, and on the recommendation of the Minister of Commerce, makes the following regulations.

Contents

Schedule 1

Application to be registered as financial service provider: Prescribed information

Schedule 2

Registration of financial service provider and contents of register: Prescribed information

Schedule 3

Annual confirmation: Prescribed information

Regulations

1 Title

These regulations are the Financial Service Providers (Registration) Regulations 2010.

2 Commencement

These regulations come into force on 16 August 2010.

3 Interpretation

In these regulations,—

Act means the Financial Service Providers (Registration and Dispute Resolution) Act 2008

FMA levies table means the levies table in the Schedule of the Financial Markets Authority (Levies) Regulations 2012

total managed assets has the meaning given in regulation 7 of the Financial Markets Authority (Levies) Regulations 2012.

4 Application to be registered as financial service provider: prescribed information

The information in Schedule 1 is prescribed for the purposes of section 15(1)(d) of the Act.

5 Registration of financial service provider and contents of register: prescribed information

The information in Schedule 2 is prescribed for the purposes of sections 16(1)(a)(iv) and 27(d) of the Act.

6 Operation of and access to register: prescribed reasons

The following are prescribed, for the purposes of section 25(3)(b) of the Act, as reasons for the Registrar to refuse access to the register or suspend its operation, in whole or in part:

(a) to enable the maintenance of the register:

(b) in response to technical difficulties in the maintenance or operation of the register:

(c) to ensure the security or integrity of the register.

7 Annual confirmation: prescribed information

The information in Schedule 3 is prescribed for the purposes of section 28(2)(c) of the Act.

8 Registrar must amend register in certain circumstances

The Registrar must amend the register if a licensing authority informs the Registrar that—

(a) a licensed provider's licence has been suspended; or

(b) a licensed provider's licence has ceased to be suspended; or

(c) a previously licensed provider has ceased to be a licensed provider.

9 Sharing information with other persons or bodies: prescribed agencies

The following agencies are prescribed for the purposes of section 34(4)(e) of the Act:

(a) the Department of Internal Affairs:

(b) the Reserve Bank of New Zealand:

(c) the Securities Commission.

Schedule 1

Application to be registered as financial service provider: Prescribed information

1 If the applicant is an individual or a corporation sole,—

(a) the applicant's residential address:

(b) any former names of the applicant:

(c) any aliases used by the applicant:

(d) the applicant's date of birth:

(e) the applicant's gender.

2 If the applicant is a body corporate that is incorporated in New Zealand, the applicant's registered office address.

3 If the applicant is a body corporate that is not incorporated in New Zealand,—

(a) the country or jurisdiction in which the applicant is incorporated:

(b) any unique identifier given to the applicant on incorporation (such as its company registration number).

4 If the applicant is a body corporate or an unincorporated body,—

(a) in relation to each director, senior manager, and controlling owner of the applicant who is an individual, the director's, senior manager's, or controlling owner's—

(i) name:

(ii) residential address:

(iii) date of birth:

(iv) gender:

(b) in relation to each director and controlling owner of the applicant that is a body corporate,—

i) the director's or controlling owner's name:

(ii) the director's or controlling owner's registered office address:

(iii) if the director or controlling owner is not incorporated in New Zealand, the country or jurisdiction in which the director or controlling owner is incorporated:

(iv) any unique identifier given to the director or controlling owner on incorporation (such as its company registration number).

5 Any trading names used by the applicant.

6 The financial services to be provided by the applicant.

7 If the applicant is not required to be a member of an approved dispute resolution scheme or the reserve scheme under section 20E of the Financial Advisers Act 2008,—

(a) the name of the person referred to in that section on behalf of whose business the applicant intends to provide a financial adviser service; and

(b) the name and business address of the approved dispute resolution scheme or reserve scheme (as the case may be) of which that person is a member.

8 A physical address in New Zealand at which the Registrar may contact the applicant (unless the business address provided under section 15(1)(a)(i) of the Act is a physical address in New Zealand).

9 An email address at which the Registrar may contact the applicant.

Schedule 2

Registration of financial service provider and contents of register: Prescribed information

1 Any trading names used by the registered financial service provider.

2 If the registered financial service provider is an individual or a corporation sole,—

(a) any former names of the registered financial service provider:

(b) any aliases used by the registered financial service provider.

3 If the registered financial service provider is a body corporate that is not incorporated in New Zealand, the country or jurisdiction in which the registered financial service provider is incorporated.

4 If the registered financial service provider is a licensed provider,—

(a) the date on which the licence expires (if supplied by the licensing authority):

(b) whether or not the licence is suspended:

(c) whether or not any conditions are imposed on the licence:

(d) details of the conditions (if any) that are imposed on the licence (if requested by the licensing authority).

5 The unique identifier issued to the registered financial service provider by the Registrar.

Schedule 3

Annual confirmation: Prescribed information

1 The registered financial service provider's name.

2 The registered financial service provider's business address.

3 If the registered financial service provider is a member of an approved dispute resolution scheme, the name and business address of the approved dispute resolution scheme.

4 If the registered financial service provider is a member of the reserve scheme, the name and business address of the reserve scheme.

5 If the registered financial service provider is not required to be a member of an approved dispute resolution scheme or the reserve scheme under section 20E of the Financial Advisers Act 2008,—

(a) the name of the person referred to in that section on behalf of whose business the registered financial provider provides a financial adviser service; and

(b) the name and business address of the approved dispute resolution scheme or reserve scheme (as the case may be) of which that person is a member.

6 If the registered financial service provider is an individual or a corporation sole,—

(a) the registered financial service provider's residential address:

(b) any former names of the registered financial service provider:

(c) any aliases used by the registered financial service provider.

7 If the registered financial service provider is a body corporate or an unincorporated body,—

(a) in relation to each director, senior manager, and controlling owner of the registered financial service provider who is an individual, the director's, senior manager's, or controlling owner's—

(i) name:

(ii) residential address:

(iii) date of birth:

(iv) gender:

(b) in relation to each director and controlling owner of the registered financial service provider that is a body corporate,—

(i) the director's or controlling owner's name:

(ii) the director's or controlling owner's registered office address:

(iii) if the director or controlling owner is not incorporated in New Zealand, the country or jurisdiction in which the director or controlling owner is incorporated:

(iv) any unique identifier given to the director or controlling owner on incorporation (such as its company registration number).

8 Any trading names used by the registered financial service provider.

9 The type or types of financial service for which the registered financial service provider is registered.

10 A physical address in New Zealand at which the Registrar may contact the registered financial service provider (unless the business address provided under clause 2 is a physical address in New Zealand).

11 An email address at which the Registrar may contact the registered financial service provider.

12 The class or classes of specified persons (as described in column 2 of the FMA levies table) that include the registered financial service provider.

13 The information (if any) required to determine the amount of levy payable by a person in a class described in clause 12 (see column 5 of the FMA levies table).

14 If the registered financial service provider is included in class 5 (as described in column 2 of the FMA levies table), the total managed assets of the registered financial service provider.

15 If the registered financial service provider is a person to whom, and is in a class and a group to which, regulation 12 of the Financial Markets Authority (Levies) Regulations 2012 applies, the financial service registration number of whichever person in the class will pay the levy on behalf of the group.

FEEDBACK

Questions?

Comments?

Please Share!

readers@michaelmagnusson.com

Follow Michael Magnusson on Twitter for Offshore Banking and Tax Haven News:

@magnussonwrites

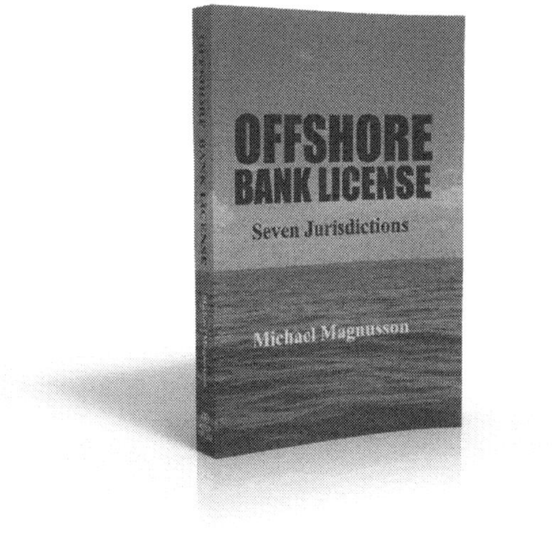

Offshore Bank License by Michael Magnusson

Regulatory changes during the early years of this millennium left merely a few Offshore Tax Havens that still welcome applications for new International Bank Licenses. Many jurisdictions have stopped accepting new applications altogether while others have decided to issue licenses exclusively to overseas branches and subsidiaries of internationally established banking groups. This book contains a compilation of banking laws and regulations from seven offshore jurisdictions that welcome new private bank startups and offer reasonable qualification and capital requirements. Minimum capital requirements start as low as $25K for a restricted Class B Banking License and from $250K for an unrestricted international license. Information is included about license classes, physical presence requirements and application procedure along with contact information for the regulatory authorities in each jurisdiction.

ISBN-10: 0957543808 – Paperback — 390 pages
Published by Opus Operis — United Kingdom

Available through all major booksellers worldwide

43726178R00133

Made in the USA
San Bernardino, CA
24 December 2016